Have Your Cake and Eat It

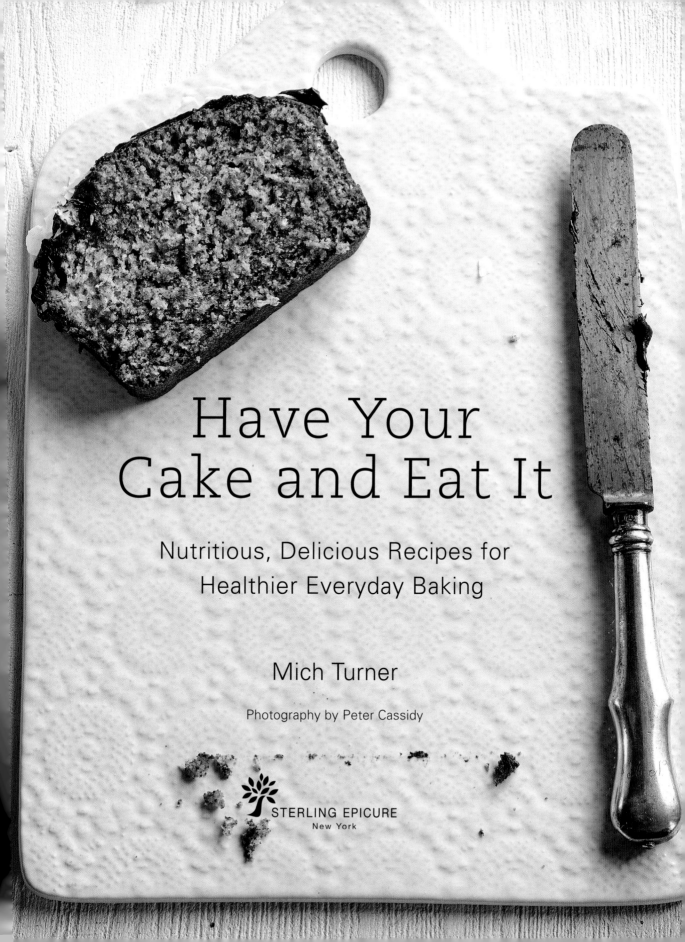

Have Your Cake and Eat It

Nutritious, Delicious Recipes for Healthier Everyday Baking

Mich Turner

Photography by Peter Cassidy

STERLING EPICURE
New York

STERLING EPICURE

New York

An Imprint of Sterling Publishing Co., Inc.
1166 Avenue of the Americas
New York, NY 10036

First published in the United Kingdom in 2017 by Jacqui Small LLP

Text © 2017 by Mich Turner
Photography © 2017 by Jacqui Small LLP

ISBN 978-1-4549-2306-0

Distributed in Canada by Sterling Publishing Co., Inc.
c/o Canadian Manda Group, 664 Annette Street Toronto, Ontario, Canada M6S 2C8

For information about custom editions, special sales, and premium and corporate purchases, please contact Sterling Special Sales at 800-805-5489 or specialsales@sterlingpublishing.com.

Manufactured in China

10 9 8 7 6 5 4 3 2 1

www.sterlingpublishing.com

Photography by Peter Cassidy
Prop Styling by Rebecca Newport

Contents

NUTRITION TAG KEY
Specific nutrition qualities
are highlighted on relevant
recipes to provide an at-a-
glance snapshot of important
nutrition benefits.

GF gluten-free

DF dairy-free

F good source of fiber

● lower fat

EF egg-free

Introduction

Baking brings a huge amount of pleasure to those who are baking, those who are receiving, and those who are sharing—but it can be a minefield to know what to bake and how to bake successfully so you can enjoy eating cake without feeling guilty.

I made my very first wedding cake 30 years ago, and have made, baked, and decorated over 10,000 cakes since then. I have always said a cake should be a feast for the eyes and a memory for the palate. As a qualified food scientist, former bakery and patisserie buyer, industry consultant, and TV judge I never tire of innovation—adapting recipes and formulating new ones to find the very best, most delicious, nutritious recipes to bake, present, and share.

In this book I want to give you choices. I am a strong advocate of using ingredients in season, with provenance, and the very best quality for maximum flavor and texture. It is so true that a cake can only be as good as its ingredients, and subtle changes can dramatically enhance and alter its characteristics.

I have included recipes with added nutrition, such as fresh and dried fruits, nuts, and seeds, featuring alternatives for gluten, fats, sugars and dairy to accommodate your personal diet and lifestyle. Ultimately, every recipe has to be delicious and I will guide you through the different baking skill levels from complete novice to experienced baker—offering practical tips and hints to ensure each and every cake is baked to success.

This book is not intended as a health or diet book. I do use butter, sugar, and cream, but I will steer you through the nutritional benefits and comparisons of these ingredients and recipes, giving you options so you can choose which cakes to bake for which occasion. I have included gluten free, dairy free, fat free, lower fat, lower sugar, lighter, more nutritious recipes that are in no way bland or boring.

This book is for those who like to bake or who aspire to be able to bake and for those who like to eat or would like to eat cake in moderation and with the knowledge that it is as nutritious and wholesome as possible.

Ingredients

It is a fact that a cake can only be as good as the ingredients you use. However, the good news is any baked treat can be improved and enhanced with the careful selection and inclusion of delicious and nutritious ingredients. As a qualified food scientist and nutritionist I hope to expel some myths and highlight the nutritional benefits of many ingredients used in this book to help you have your cake and eat it.

Cakes and other baked goods are essentially made up of carbohydrate or starch (such as flour to absorb the moisture and set the structure); eggs to bind, stabilize, and aerate; fat to carry the flavor, provide mouthfeel, and prolong freshness; and sugar, which adds sweetness.

Within these categories there are many variations that will play a pivotal role, and there are many other additions such as fresh or dried fruits, vegetables, nuts, spices, and chocolate from nature's own bounty to enhance your baking and add nutritional benefit.

It is important to remember that these treats should be included as part of a wider healthier diet and not consumed in total isolation!

LEFT Frozen fruits can be used to make a fabulous fruit compote out of season. Add orange zest for added flavor.

Fats

Fats can be derived from vegetable or animal sources and yield the highest amount of energy—9 calories per gram.

The body can synthesize most of the fats it needs from diet. However, there are two essential fatty acids—linoleic and alpha-linoleic acid—that cannot be synthesized and must be ingested from food. These essential acids are so called because they are required for normal, healthy, function of many biological processes, including mood enhancers, reducing inflammation, and healthy nerve function. A lack of essential fatty acids could lead to dermatitis and poor skin healing. There is also evidence that low levels, or an imbalance of these essential fatty acids may be a factor in osteoporosis. Sources of these essential fatty acids include flaxseeds, olive oil, soybean oil, canola oil, chia seeds, pumpkin seeds, and sunflower seeds.

Fats can be trans, saturated, monounsaturated, or polyunsaturated. Mono- and polyunsaturated fats are fats found in nuts, nut butters, seeds, and seed oils to provide essential fatty acids and fat-soluble vitamins A,D, E, and K. They can be consumed in smaller quantities, where they help to maintain healthy cholesterol levels.

Saturated fats include butter, whole milk, cream, and coconut oil. They are more stable when heated than other fats, and should be consumed in moderation, as they can increase the amount of cholesterol in the diet.

Trans fats include hard vegetable margarines and hydrogenated vegetable oils. The process of hardening oils to be solid at room temperature turns them from an unsaturated to a saturated fat. The structure of the fat created (trans) is harmful to the body, increasing the LDL cholesterol.

By making and baking your own cakes and cookies you can be aware of the fats in your diet—opting to include more polyunsaturated essential fatty acids, limiting saturated fats, and avoiding trans fats altogether.

Fats include:
Butter
Sunflower, olive, canola, soybean oil
Vegan spread
Coconut oil
Nut butters—peanut, cashew, almond, hazelnut
Cream cheese
Heavy cream
Whipping cream
Sour cream
Greek yogurt
Coconut milk
Buttermilk
Cow's milk
Soy milk
Egg yolk

SUNFLOWER OIL

Sunflower oil is 100 percent vegetable fat and is suitable for vegans, vegetarians, and those following a gluten-free, dairy-free diet. It works well in batter cakes or those made by the melted method, as it is liquid at room temperature, which helps to keep the cake moist. Look for high-quality cold-pressed or organic sunflower oil.

COCONUT OIL

Coconut oil is 100 percent saturated fat, but contains mid-length triglycerides that are thought to provide better health and nutritional benefits. Coconut oil contains no cholesterol and is a good choice for a non-dairy diet.

Coconut milk

Peanut butter

Cream cheese

Greek yogurt

Heavy cream

Buttermilk

Sunflower oil

Coconut oil

Unsalted butter

Vegan margarine

BUTTER

Made from churned cream, butter must contain a minimum of 80 percent fat. It is a saturated fat, but not a trans fat, therefore it is more stable, when heated, and can be metabolized in the body. I use unsalted butter in all my baking, which offers a fresh, creamier, distinctive flavor that is not salty. Salted butter will have a longer shelf life as salt is a preservative. Butter contains calcium as well as fat soluble vitamins.

VEGAN MARGARINE OR SPREAD

To be used successfully in baking, look for vegetable margarines that contain a minimum of 80 percent fat. Avoid spreads, as they will affect your baking. Look specifically for a NON-TRANS fat, as these oils have to be hydrogenated in some way to be solid at room temperature.

COCONUT MILK

Made by soaking grated coconut flesh in hot water. Coconut milk is rich in fiber, water-soluble B vitamins and minerals, including iron, selenium, sodium, calcium, magnesium, and phosphorous for healthy metabolism and bones. Unlike cow's milk, coconut milk does not contain lactose and can be used by those following a lactose-free or dairy-free diet.

PEANUT BUTTER

An excellent source of protein, fiber, and B vitamins, as well as iron and potassium. Both crunchy and smooth, nut butters are sources of saturated and unsaturated fats. Made by crushing the roasted nuts to a paste. Be sure to choose the no added salt or sugar varieties.

CREAM CHEESE

A soft cheese made from cream and milk, usually made with a stabilizer, such as locust bean gum. It is 34 percent fat, providing 342 calories per 3½ ounces and 110mg cholesterol per 3½ ounces. At 34 percent fat, versus the 80 percent fat of butter, cream cheese frostings can offer a good lower fat frosting.

GREEK YOGURT

Full-fat greek yogurt contains just 9 percent fat and 116 calories per 3½ ounces. It should have a live culture, offering beneficial microflora and no added sugar. Lower or 0 percent fat yogurts will have less fat-soluble vitamins, may have added sugar, and will be less creamy and lack flavor.

HEAVY CREAM

This type of cream is 48 percent fat and can be boiled, whipped, or frozen. Always be careful when whipping heavy cream—it can be overwhipped very easily, turning grainy and eventually splitting into butter and buttermilk. Extra thick heavy cream is recommended for whipped toppings, as the cream has been homogenized (the fat globules have been evenly distributed).

WHIPPING CREAM

This is a lighter version of heavy cream with a fat content of over 35 percent—the minimum amount necessary to allow it to stay firm once beaten or whipped. The fat globules encase the air, when whisked, and provide the characteristic texture of whipped cream. Whipping cream whips well, and is less rich than heavy cream.

SOUR CREAM

A light cream (20 percent fat) that's been soured using an added culture (similar to that used in yogurt). It is not suitable for whipping, so I use it to fill cakes or in frostings.

BUTTERMILK

This is the liquid that remains after the butter has been separated from milk or cream. With only 40 calories per 3½ ounces and less than 1 percent fat, I tend to use buttermilk in scones as the lactic acidity in the buttermilk activates the raising agent.

Flours & Carbohydrates

Carbohydrates provide 4 calories per 3½ ounces, but, more importantly in baking, offer structural support to baked cakes. The starch granules swell during the baking process until they burst and absorb the liquid. As baking continues, the starch sets and the baked cake will stabilize. Correct temperature, accurate measurements, and adhering to bake times will help ensure that cakes are baked correctly.

Wheat flour contains the proteins glutenin and gliadin. When these come into contact with liquid, they form the elasticated protein gluten, responsible for achieving the lift in cakes and breads. Many people choose to avoid gluten if they have a food intolerance, or feel better when limiting or excluding it from their diet. For those suffering from celiac disease, which is an autoimmune disease, gluten must be avoided.

Other grains such as rye, oats, and barley also contain gluten—in lower quantities.

Many carbohydrates, other than the obvious wheat flour, can be used in baking. These include:

All-purpose flour (gluten)
Whole wheat flour (gluten)
Spelt flour (lower gluten)
Gluten-free flour
Cornmeal
Cornstarch
Popping corn
Oats (lower gluten)
Gluten-free oats
Steel-cut oats (Irish oats, Scotch oats)
Ground almonds
Cocoa powder

FLOURS
Barley & spelt flours (an ancient variety of wheat) can be substituted in part for wheat flour to add texture and flavor, but are less readily available, and will give different results, as they are lower in gluten.

Whole wheat flour contains all of the wheat grain and offers additional nutrition. This flour works well in melting method cakes, where there is a lot of moisture and strong flavors from spices and sugars. Cakes made with whole wheat flour tend to be more dense, with less aeration, and require more moisture before baking; but can offer a greater depth of flavor and texture.

Cornstarch is used very much as a thickening agent in baking. It is finely ground corn flour, and is gluten free.

Wheat flour provides the best result for cakes —light, aerated with sufficient starch, and protein to support the cake and absorb moisture during baking. Cakes should be made with all-purpose wheat flour, which is lower in gluten, and never with bread flour, which is much higher in gluten and will result in tough, chewy, dense cakes.

All-purpose flour is pure wheat flour with no raising agents added.

Self-rising flour has baking powder already included in the flour.

Gluten-free flour can be milled from rice, corn, tapioca, buckwheat, or potato and can be substituted successfully in cake baking, where the recipe requires a lower percentage of flour by design, and has other strong flavors included—such as chocolate, spices, or molasses. The effect of using gluten-free flour tends to be

Popcorn

Oats

Ground almonds

Oatmeal

Coconut flour

Cornmeal

Spelt

Whole wheat flour

Cornstarch

Self-rising flour

Plain wheat flour

Gluten-free flour

more crumbly with a gritty texture and a stronger aftertaste. Xanthan gum can be added to cakes made with gluten-free flour to improve the crumb structure and reduce crumbling.

Coconut flour is gluten-free and high in fiber with a distinctive, earthy flavor. I tend to use it in conjunction with wheat flour, rather than by itself, otherwise the results can be quite dry.

POPCORN

Popping corn is added to a pan of hot oil. The kernels expand and puff up until the pressure builds sufficiently to "pop" the corn. Gluten-free and containing lots of air, 3½ ounces kernels will go a long way and provide 382 calories with just 4g fat. The kernels are a notable source of B vitamins and iron.

CORNMEAL

Cornmeal is gluten-free ground corn. It is less than 1 percent fat, with 0 percent cholesterol. It offers a grainy texture to baked goods.

OATMEAL

Steel-cut oats or whole oat groats are the inner kernel of the whole oats, which have been roughly chopped, offering a chewier, nutty-flavored oat than rolled oats. (Steel-cut oats are also known as Irish oats, Scotch oats, and pinhead oats.)

OATS

Oats are generally considered healthy as they are a good source of protein, fiber, and B vitamins. They offer slow-release energy and thanks to their beta glucans have been proven to lower cholesterol.

GROUND ALMONDS

Made from ground sweet blanched almonds. Gluten free and rich in polyunsaturated fats.

RAISING AGENTS & CHEMICALS

Raising agents (leavening agents) go hand in hand with carbohydrates and can be obtained gluten-free.

Baking soda is a powerful chemical leavening agent that reacts with acids such as vinegar, buttermilk, yogurt, or lemon juice to produce carbon dioxide, which helps baked goods rise. It works well with batter cakes and stronger flavors.

Baking powder is a more gentle raising agent for softer, lighter, more subtle-flavored cakes.

Cream of tartar stabilizes egg whites, increasing their heat resistance and maximizing volume, when making meringues or chiffon-style cakes.

Vinegar reacts with baking soda to produce carbon dioxide as a powerful raising agent. Use this mix of ingredients right away.

Sugars

Sugars have come in for some negative press in light of their link to obesity, Type 2 diabetes, cardiovascular disease, and tooth decay. Sugars and syrups are necessary for baking in whatever guise you choose. They are all processed similarly within the body, requiring insulin produced in the pancreas to maintain a sugar balance in the blood.

Be sensible; use natural sources of sugar derived from fruits and dairy products, which will add nutritional benefits of fiber, vitamins, and minerals, and thereby will enable you to reduce added sugars. Be aware of refined versus unrefined sugars. Offering no difference in nutritional value, unrefined sugars have enhanced flavor and trace elements that have more flavor, rather than just being sweet. Some recipes, however, will benefit from refined sugar, visually—and I have clearly highlighted these so you can choose to use alternatives if you wish. Encourage yourself to enjoy the flavor of your baked goods rather than just the sweetness.

Sugar offers 4 calories per gram and can be categorized into monosaccharides, disaccharides, and oligosaccharides. Monosaccharides are the simplest of sugars and include glucose, galactose, and fructose (fruit sugar). Disaccharides include sucrose, also known as common table sugar, such as granulated, superfine, and powdered sugar (made up of glucose and fructose monosaccharides) and lactose (milk sugar—made up of glucose and galactose monosaccharides). Oligosaccharides are made up of chains of these simple sugars and are found in many fruits and vegetables.

Sugars include:

Powdered sugar

Demerara sugar

Granulated sugar

Superfine sugar

Soft light brown sugar

Soft dark brown sugar

Muscovado sugar

Maple syrup

Honey

Corn syrup (light corn syrup)

Molasses

Citrus curds (see page 18)

Fruit compote (see page 19)

The main difference between white and brown (raw) sugar is that the brown (raw) sugar hasn't been completely refined. Raw brown sugar contains a small percentage of molasses, with trace amounts of the minerals calcium, potassium, iron, and magnesium. The darker the sugar the more molasses the sugar will contain—between 5–10 percent. Molasses adds to the darker color and flavor of brown sugar.

TOP TIP

The body metabolizes carbohydrates into simple sugars. The brain uses glucose as its sole energy source. A good reason to eat cake!

Molasses sugar

Maple syrup

Treacle (used in the UK)

Dark muscovado sugar

Honey

Molasses

Demerara sugar

Granulated sugar

Light soft brown sugar

Corn syrup

Superfine sugar

Golden superfine sugar
(used in the UK)

Golden powdered sugar
(used in the UK)

Powdered sugar

Glucose syrup
(used in the UK)

Citrus Curds

Citrus curds, using fresh lemon, lime, orange, or passion fruit are wonderful by themselves or stirred into buttercreams for a zesty filling. These work really well injected into cupcakes and muffins for extra flavor, texture, and color.

 GF

ALL CURDS MAKE ABOUT 19–21 OUNCES

FOR LEMON CURD

4 lemons, rind and juice

1¾ cups superfine sugar

4 eggs, beaten

½ cup/1 stick unsalted butter, chilled and cubed

FOR ORANGE CURD

1 large orange, rind and juice

juice of 2 lemons

scant 1½ cups superfine sugar

3 eggs, plus 1 egg yolk, beaten

½ cup/1 stick unsalted butter, chilled and cubed

FOR PASSION FRUIT CURD

8 passion fruits, cut in half and flesh and seeds scooped out

juice of 1 lemon

generous 1 cup superfine sugar

3 medium eggs, plus 1 egg yolk, beaten

⅓ cup/¾ stick unsalted butter, chilled and cubed

FOR LIME CURD

2 limes, rind and juice

2 medium lemons, rind and juice

generous 1 cup superfine sugar

3 medium eggs, plus 1 egg yolk, beaten

⅓ cup/¾ stick unsalted butter, cubed

1 Place the citrus rind or passion fruit flesh and seeds in a saucepan together with the juice, sugar, eggs, and butter. Heat over medium-low heat, stirring all the time. Do not let the curd boil. As it gradually thickens it will begin to coat the back of a wooden spoon.

2 Remove from the heat and strain through a fine metal strainer.

Store for up to 4 weeks in clean jars in the refrigerator.

TOP TIPS

- The curd should be heated until it thickens to ensure the eggs are hot enough to cook the curd, making it safe and stable.
- Do not let the curd boil, as this will damage the delicate protein structure of the eggs and the curd will scramble and be rubbery.
- Blending the eggs really well before adding them helps to stabilize.

Fruit Berry Compote

Fresh fruit berry compotes are a natural way to add flavor, interest, texture, and nutrition to your baked goods. They can be stirred into cake batters before baking; added to buttercreams to naturally color and flavor them; spread between layers, or onto meringues and pavlovas; or injected into muffins and cupcakes for a fruity hit.

Use fruits when they are in season, or frozen berries throughout the year. As the fruits are heat treated and combined with sugar, they will keep for up to 14 days in the refrigerator, and can be frozen in small containers for up to 3 months. Defrost thoroughly before using.

MAKES ABOUT 18 OUNCES

4½ cups fresh or frozen fruit (strawberries, raspberries, blackcurrants, blackberries)
½ cup superfine sugar
grated zest and juice of 1 lemon or orange (optional)

1 Place the fruit, sugar, and citrus zest and juice, if using, together in a heavy-based saucepan over medium heat and bring to a gentle simmer. Continue to heat, stirring occasionally, for about 25–30 minutes until the fruit has softened and reduced to a thick pulp.

2 Remove from the heat. Taste and adjust the sugar or add lemon juice to taste.

Store for up to 14 days in an airtight container in the refrigerator.

TOP TIP
The fruit should simmer gently, but not to a rolling boil, as this can burn and damage the flavor of the fruit.

Other Ingredients

In order for my baked goods to have added nutrition and be utterly delicious, I have chosen to include nature's best ingredients in the form of nuts, seeds, spices, fruit, and vegetables.

FRUIT
Fresh, dried, or frozen, there is an abundance of fruit that can be used in baking to provide natural sweetness, fiber, vitamins, minerals, flavor, texture, and color. Many dried fruits provide a concentrated source of these nutrients to have a significant benefit to boosting the daily intake of essential vitamins and minerals.

Dried fruits include apricots, prunes, figs, dates, raisins, cherries, cranberries, raisins, and currants. Make sure you choose unsweetened varieties.

Fresh fruits include berries, apples, pears, pineapple, bananas, peaches, plums, nectarines, apricots, and citrus fruits. Choose fruits when they are in season and buy local when you can.

Frozen fruits are a great choice for fruit compotes. They can be easily stored and used any time throughout the year. They are picked and frozen when they are most ripe, usually making them a less expensive and more convenient way to obtain them.

FRESH VEGETABLES
Carrots, pumpkins, beets, parsnips, and zucchini can be used in baking to add moisture, dietary fiber, and nutritional vitamins and minerals to cakes. They are generally lower in simple sugars and have little, if any, fat.

NUTS
All nuts can be used in baking to add protein, essential fats, minerals, and vitamins as well as flavor and texture. Roasting

nuts beforehand can intensify their flavor and crunch by driving off some of the oil. Always use fresh, unsalted nuts. My favorites include cashews, almonds, walnuts, pecans, pine nuts, hazelnuts, macadamias, and pistachios. They are often interchangeable, so experiment to find your favorites.

SEEDS
Pumpkin, sunflower, chia, flaxseed, and poppy seeds will provide powerful energy, antioxidants, essential oils, and vitamins and minerals. A little go a long way and offer an alternative to nuts. Add a handful to crumbles, loaf cakes, and muffins to boost the overall nutritional content.

SPICES
Fresh ginger has a wonderful mellow, fragrant, and distinctive flavor that can enhance many baked goods. Spices such as cinnamon, nutmeg, and allspice are good pantry staples.

VANILLA
The most versatile natural flavor is vanilla—taken from the root of the vanilla orchid plant. The seeds have a distinctive and potent flavor and come in a variety of forms—from vanilla beans, powder, extract, and paste. Be sure to choose the real thing and avoid vanilla flavor or flavoring.

EGGS
An essential ingredient in baking. The egg white (albumen) is an elasticated protein that provides aeration to baked goods. When used at room temperature, the egg white can create a honeycomb structure of air sacs, like thousands of tiny balloons all together. The warmer the egg white, the more it can expand, the more air sacs and ultimately the more air into your cakes—leaving them super light and aerated. Using cold eggs will inhibit the amount of air that can be incorporated and your baked goods will not be as light and aerated as they could be.

Egg yolk contains a powerful emulsifier—lecithin. This emulsifier will stabilize an emulsion (water and oil), as well as stabilize the batter.

Eggs are delicate structures, they like to be added slowly and like to be warm. They act as a binding agent and offer protein, essential fats, and nutrients. A word of caution though—egg yolk is very high in cholesterol—one large egg yolk contains approximately 180mg cholesterol. The recommended daily allowance is 300mg (or 200mg if you are considered high risk).

Chocolate

Chocolate is produced from fermenting, drying, cleaning, and roasting cocoa beans. Once the shell is removed, the cocoa nibs are ground to cocoa mass. This mass is liquefied into cocoa solids and cocoa butter.

I generally use a dark chocolate with 70 percent cocoa solids—this is made primarily of cocoa solids and cocoa butter, with very little added sugar and no added milk. This chocolate has the nutritional benefits of fiber, iron, magnesium, copper, manganese, potassium, phosphorus, zinc, and selenium, and can be appropriate for those following a dairy-free diet.

The fat in this dark chocolate may have a beneficial effect on cholesterol levels, as it consists mainly of stearic and oleic acid. While stearic acid is a saturated fat, it is unlike other saturated fats, as it does not raise blood cholesterol levels. Oleic acid is a monounsaturated acid, which does not raise cholesterol levels and may even reduce it.

Dark chocolate & cocoa contain powerful antioxidants to protect against aging, cardiovascular disease, and encourage cell regeneration.

Semi-sweet chocolate is a combination of cocoa solids, cocoa butter (or possibly vegetable fat), and sugar.

Milk chocolate contains milk powder, or condensed milk, and is not suitable for those following a dairy-free diet.

White chocolate contains cocoa butter, sugar, and milk, but none of the beneficial cocoa solids.

The lower the cocoa solids, the greater the sugar and added fat and fewer beneficial nutritional effects.

Drinking chocolate contains mostly sugar with cocoa powder, salt, and flavoring. The cocoa solids are usually around 25 percent. I have only used this in my recipe to dust Chocolate-dusted Orange Madeleines (see page 52).

Cocoa   Drinking chocolate   Milk chocolate

Dark chocolate   White chocolate   51% semi-sweet chocolate

Cake dos and don'ts

As a food scientist I am aware of the chemistry when I am making and baking cakes. To become a better baker, it helps to understand what to do and why you are doing it.

FRESH INGREDIENTS
It is imperative to use the freshest ingredients, of the highest quality. Buy fresh, use fresh, and don't compromise.

WEIGH ACCURATELY
Baking is a science, relying on delicate interactions between ingredients. Invest in a set of digital scales and measuring spoons to accurately measure all dry and wet ingredients. Don't rely on guesswork and annotate any changes you make to a recipe so you can remember for another time.

TEMPERATURE
Most ingredients work best at room temperature —including butter, sugar, flour, and eggs. Butter will cream better and eggs will whisk better. Take the ingredients out of the refrigerator the night before you are intending to bake. Don't be tempted to warm butter in the microwave—it will just melt and then not be suitable for creaming. Eggs will pasteurize when the temperature reaches between 142–158°F. Invest in a digital thermometer to accurately measure temperature to ensure eggs and syrups are safe and stable.

PREHEATING THE OVEN
Preheat the oven to the correct temperature before placing cakes in the oven. This will ensure the batter quickly reaches the desired temperature to achieve the physical changes necessary during baking. Too low, and the cake ingredients will melt before being baked, resulting in a soggy, sunken, pale cake. Too high, and the cake surface and sides will color, burn, and dry out long before the center of the cake is baked. Use oven gloves to protect yourself in the kitchen.

CORRECT UTENSILS
• Use the right tool for the task.
• Beating and creaming should be done with a wooden spoon, an electric hand mixer, or a stand mixer fitted with a beater attachment.
• Folding should be done with a metal spoon or rubber spatula.
• Whisking should be done with a balloon whisk, an electric hand mixer, or a stand mixer fitted with a whisk attachment.
• Graters, microplanes, zesters, peelers, rubber spatulas, scissors, and knives will all help maximize your efficiency.

CORRECT SIZED PANS & LINING
Measure pans to ensure you are using the size stated in the recipe. This will ensure the batter fits the pan and bakes according to the recipe. Line pans with parchment paper or grease them with melted butter, or not at all (e.g. for chiffon cakes)

UNDERSTAND PHYSICAL CHEMISTRY TERMINOLOGY
Rubbing in—combining fat eith dry ingredients, either with your fingertips (if you have cold hands) or with an electric mixer fitted with a paddle attachment. The idea is not to melt the butter as it is distributed in small granules through the dry ingredient.

Creaming—beating the fat and sugar together to create a light, aerated emulsion. It is not possible to over-cream—so turn the electric mixer on and leave it on for a good 10 minutes.

Folding—carefully distributing dry ingredients into an emulsion or batter. Use a metal spoon or rubber spatula to avoid knocking out air or overworking the gluten in the flour. Both would result in a dense, tough, chewy cake.

Beating—blending ingredients together but not necessarily to aerate. Use a wooden spoon or electric mixer fitted with a paddle attachment.

Melting—the process of turning a solid to liquid.
- Butter—melt in the microwave or in a small saucepan over medium heat.
- Chocolate—melt in a bowl suspended over a pan of gently simmering water or in a bowl in the microwave with medium heat being careful not to burn the chocolate.

Whisking—using a hand-held whisk or stand mixer fitted with a whisk attachment. The act of adding air to cream or eggs to achieve a highly aerated foam. Avoid fat or grease in the bowl. Wash it in hot soapy water, rinse, and dry it with paper towels.
- Eggs can be whisked to a frothy, soft peak or firm peak stage.
- Cream should be carefully whipped and not be granular.
- Eggs and sugar for whisking or meringues should be light, even, and frothy, with a velvety appearance.

Caramelizing versus burning—sugar will pass through a series of changes from light thread syrup to a burned mess, as it heats from 212 to 392°F. Heat slowly and carefully.

PATIENCE
The most important quality to be a successful baker is patience. Allow yourself plenty of time to make a cake—perfection cannot be rushed, and understanding all these principles will help you develop into a successful, confident baker.

SUGAR TEMPERATURES

NAME	TEMPERATURE	TOUCH / VISUAL TEST	USE
Syrup/Thread	223–234°F	Coats a spoon	Basic stock syrup —as used in vanilla cake
Soft ball	234–240°F	Forms a soft ball when rolled	Jams and jellies —fruit compote
Firm ball	242–248°F	Forms a firm ball when rolled	Italian meringue
Hard ball	250–266°F	Forms a hard ball that holds its shape	Marshmallows
Soft crack	270–290°F	Will not roll and will show small cracks as sets	Candies
Hard crack	295–310°F	Will shatter when placed in water	Poured or pulled sugar nougat
Light caramel	311–320°F	Visually a light amber	Praline
Caramel	320–360°F	Dark brown	Praline

Muffins, Cupcakes, & More

Probably the easiest entry level when it comes to baking, as you don't need to invest in a huge amount of equipment, time, or skill to achieve fantastic baked results. These are a great and fun way to inspire beginners and children—to learn about ingredients, the baking process, flavors, textures, and decoration. I have included scones, madeleines, tea cakes, and cupcakes to stretch your imagination and skill, and have been mindful of dietary requirements to offer you healthier choices for everyday baking.

Date, Banana, & Peanut Butter Muffins

MAKES 12 MUFFINS

2½ cups ripe mashed bananas (about 4 large bananas)

½ cup sunflower oil

1 teaspoon vanilla bean paste

½ cup crunchy peanut butter

1 egg, beaten

2⅔ cups all-purpose flour

scant ⅔ cup soft light brown sugar

1 teaspoon baking powder

1 teaspoon baking soda

1⅔ cups chopped dates or figs

3 tablespoons mixed sunflower and pumpkin seeds, plus extra for sprinkling

These delicious dairy-free cakes are baked in individual baking cups so they are perfectly portioned. Relatively low in fat, the flavor is all in the banana, with texture from the peanut butter, dates, and seeds. They are nutritious and wholesome with natural sugar, high fiber, vitamins, and nutrients in the dried fruits, nuts, and seeds. I like to have a batch of these available for mid-morning second breakfasts —they are also great for a school or office lunch box.

1 Preheat the oven to 350°F. Line a muffin pan with 12 fluted baking cups.

2 Mash the bananas in a large bowl with the sunflower oil, vanilla bean paste, peanut butter, and beaten egg.

3 In a separate bowl, stir together the flour, sugar, baking powder, and baking soda. Add the chopped dates or figs and seeds and toss to coat.

4 Add the flour mixture to the banana mixture and stir until just combined.

5 Divide the batter between the 12 baking cups and sprinkle with seeds. Bake for 20 minutes until golden. Let cool for 5 minutes before transferring to a wire rack.

Store for 2–3 days in an airtight container in the refrigerator. Not suitable for freezing.

MUFFINS, CUPCAKES, & MORE

These muffins are packed with fresh peach and raspberries and injected with fruit compote for natural added sweetness and flavor. They are dairy free, making them the perfect choice for breakfast or a mid-morning snack.

Peach Melba Muffins

 DF F

MAKES 12 MUFFINS

1½ cups all-purpose flour

scant ½ cup ground almonds

1 teaspoon baking powder

generous ½ cup superfine sugar

2 eggs

generous ⅓ cup sunflower oil

generous 1 cup soy or coconut
   yogurt

2 large peaches, 1 pitted and
   chopped and 1 cut into 12 slices

8 amaretti cookies, lightly
   crushed

½ quantity Fruit Compote
   (see page 19), blended until
   smooth

scant ½ cup fresh raspberries

½ cup sliced almonds

1 Preheat the oven to 350°F. Line a muffin pan with 12 baking cups.

2 Sift the flour, ground almonds, and baking powder into a bowl.

3 In a separate bowl, mix together the sugar, eggs, oil, and non-dairy yogurt. Add the flour and mix until just combined. Lightly fold in the chopped peach and crushed amaretti cookies. Spoon the batter into the cups.

4 Spoon the smooth fruit compote into a pastry bag and snip the end to make a small hole. Insert the tip just under the surface of the batter and inject about 2 teaspoons compote per muffin. Top with a peach slice, a few raspberries, and some sliced almonds.

5 Bake for 25–30 minutes before cooling on a wire rack.

Store for 2–3 days in an airtight container in the refrigerator. Not suitable for freezing.

VARIATION
If using coconut yogurt, consider substituting the ground almonds with dried unsweetened coconut.

4

LEFT "Keeping You Regular" Muffins with prunes, apricots, and figs.
RIGHT "Back to Your Roots" Muffins with carrot, parsnip, and beet.

Oats, figs, apricots, and prunes in a muffin—these will certainly help to keep you regular! Full of iron, B vitamins, and fiber, these muffins are super quick to make and will easily keep hunger at bay. I have used sunflower oil and buttermilk, added texture with the hazelnuts, and rounded the muffins off with a little cinnamon. Enjoy for breakfast or weekend brunch.

"Keeping You Regular" Muffins

MAKES 8 MUFFINS

1⅓ cups self-rising flour

½ cup oats

generous ½ cup light brown sugar

2 teaspoons ground cinnamon

½ teaspoon baking soda

1 large egg, beaten

scant ⅔ cup buttermilk

1 teaspoon vanilla extract

generous ⅓ cup sunflower oil

⅔ cup chopped and roasted
   hazelnuts

½ cup chopped prunes

½ cup chopped apricots

½ cup chopped figs

1 Preheat the oven to 350°F. Line a muffin pan with 8 baking cups.

2 Put the flour, oats, sugar, cinnamon, and baking soda in a large bowl. Stir until well mixed.

3 In a separate bowl, mix together the egg, buttermilk, vanilla, and oil. Stir into the dry ingredients to make a smooth batter. Set aside ¼ cup of the chopped hazelnuts and then fold in the chopped dried fruits and remaining hazelnuts.

4 Spoon the batter into the prepared cups and sprinkle over the reserved hazelnuts. Bake for 20–25 minutes. Serve warm or cold.

Store for 2–3 days in an airtight container at room temperature. Suitable for freezing.

Root vegetables have their own natural sweetness and contain no fat. Carrots, parsnips, and beets can all be used, depending on your personal preferences and seasonal availability. These vegetables add fiber, flavor, texture, color, vitamins, and minerals and are nature's own harvest. Because they contain so much water they help keep the muffins nice and moist. I have made these dairy-free and added coconut, with a little coconut flour, to reduce the overall gluten content. Coconut flour is gluten free, absorbs a huge amount of water (which needs to be taken into account when using it in baking) and adds a gritty, rounded flavor.

"Back to Your Roots" Muffins

MAKES 12 MUFFINS

scant 1 cup all-purpose flour

generous ⅓ cup coconut flour

2 teaspoons ground cinnamon

1 teaspoon ground nutmeg

1 teaspoon mixed spice

1 teaspoon baking soda

2 large eggs

scant ⅔ cup sunflower oil

¾ cup soft light brown sugar

grated zest of 1 orange

grated zest of 1 lemon

7 ounces grated root vegetables
(a mixture of peeled carrots,
beets, parsnips)

scant ½ cup chopped hazelnuts

1 Preheat the oven to 350°F. Line a muffin pan with 12 baking cups.

2 Sift the flours together with the spices and baking soda in a large bowl. Stir until well mixed.

3 In a separate bowl, beat together the eggs, oil, and sugar until smooth. Stir in the dry ingredients and mix to a smooth batter.

4 Fold in the remaining ingredients. Spoon the batter into the prepared cups. Bake for 25–30 minutes, and transfer to a wire rack to cool.

Store for 2–3 days in an airtight container at room temperature. Suitable for freezing.

Raspberry, Rose, & Pistachio Cupcakes

The delicate flavor, color, and texture of these cupcakes marry beautifully to create cakes that I think are perfect for bridal or baby showers. Making mini cupcakes that are packed full of flavor and texture, rather than regular size, will allow every guest to sample a cake without all the calories. Freeze-dried fruit powders add an intense flavor and sherbet fizz to the buttercream without adding moisture or the need for extra sugar or artificial colors.

4 cups fresh raspberries (or
    enough for 3 raspberries to
    be put in the bottom of each
    cupcake liner)

generous 1 cup/2¼ sticks
    unsalted butter, softened

1¼ cups superfine sugar

4 large eggs

1¾ cups self-rising flour

½ teaspoon baking powder

¼ cup whole milk

1–2 teaspoons rose water

½ cup roughly chopped
    pistachios, plus extra to
    decorate

FOR THE BUTTERCREAM

generous 1 cup/2¼ sticks
    unsalted butter, softened

3½ cups powdered sugar

2 tablespoons milk

3–4 teaspoons freeze-dried
    raspberry powder

1 Preheat the oven to 325°F. Place 18 cupcake liners in cupcake pans (or 48 mini cupcake liners in mini cupcake pans) and place 3 raspberries in the bottom of each (only use 1 raspberry if using mini cupcake liners).

2 In a large bowl, cream together the butter and sugar. Add the eggs, slowly, mixing until light and fluffy. Sift the flour and baking powder into the batter and fold in carefully. Stir in the milk, rose water, and finally, the pistachios.

3 Fill a large pastry bag with the batter, snip the end, and pipe the batter into the cupcake liners until they are two-thirds full. Bake for 15 minutes until risen and golden brown. Remove from the oven and transfer to a wire rack to cool.

4 To make the buttercream, whip the butter for 1–2 minutes until soft. Add the powdered sugar in 2 batches and whisk until fully combined. Add the milk and raspberry powder and whisk. Top each cupcake with a swirl of buttercream and decorate with chopped roasted pistachios.

Store for 2 days in an airtight container at room temperature. Not suitable for freezing.

1

3

These vegan cupcakes contain no dairy, eggs, or honey. When eggs were rationed, cakes relied on a chemical reaction between vinegar and baking soda to produce carbon dioxide, which would help the cakes rise during baking. This principle works in these vegan cupcakes, which are decorated with a vegan frosting.

Vegan Vanilla Cupcakes

MAKES 12 REGULAR-SIZED OR 18 SMALLER CUPCAKES

1½ cups superfine sugar

scant ⅔ cup sunflower oil

1 tablespoon vanilla bean paste

generous 2 cups dairy-free soy yogurt or a mix of soy, almond, and coconut yogurt

2 teaspoons white vinegar

2¾ cups all-purpose flour

1 teaspoon baking soda

1½ teaspoons baking powder

toasted coconut flakes, for sprinkling

FOR THE VEGAN VANILLA BUTTERCREAM

10½ ounces vegan or non-dairy spread (at least 80% fat)

4½ cups powdered sugar

1 tablespoon vanilla bean paste

1 Preheat the oven to 325°F. Line a muffin pan with 12 cupcake liners (or a mini muffin pan with 18 mini liners).

2 Put the sugar, oil, and vanilla in a large bowl and beat until well mixed. Blend the yogurt and vinegar together, then add to the bowl and mix well.

3 Sift together the flour, baking soda, and baking powder and add these to the cupcake batter. Stir until everything is mixed, then divide the batter between the cupcake liners until they are two-thirds full.

4 Bake for 20 minutes until risen and golden, then let cool on a wire rack.

5 To make the buttercream, beat the vegan spread for 1–2 minutes, then add the powdered sugar in 2 batches. Add the vanilla bean paste to taste. Top each cupcake with a swirl of buttercream and decorate with toasted coconut flakes.

Store for 2–3 days in an airtight container in the refrigerator. Not suitable for freezing.

VARIATION

VEGAN CHOCOLATE CUPCAKES—substitute 2 tablespoons of the all-purpose flour with cocoa powder and decorate with dairy-free chocolate buttercream (see below) and dairy-free dark chocolate decorations.

DAIRY-FREE CHOCOLATE BUTTERCREAM—heat 4 ounces dark chocolate with ⅓ cup water until melted and smooth, then mix into 1 quantity of the vanilla buttercream (see above).

The Hummingbird cake comes from Jamaica, and is named after the island's national bird. It is by nature a dairy-free cake with the added nutritional benefits of pineapple, bananas, and nuts. It is usually layered with cream cheese frosting. The recipe was created and published internationally as a marketing strategy to encourage tourists to visit the island. I love the tropical, sunshine flavors and have chosen to use a dairy-free coconut frosting.

Hummingbird Cupcakes

MAKES 20 CUPCAKES

2¾ cups all-purpose flour

2 cups superfine sugar

1 teaspoon baking soda

1 tablespoon ground cinnamon

generous 1 cup sunflower oil

3 large eggs, beaten

1 tablespoon vanilla bean paste

4 medium or 2 large very ripe
   bananas (about 1 pound)

8 ounces fresh or canned
   pineapple, crushed or finely
   chopped

¾ cup chopped pecans or walnuts

edible flowers, to decorate

**FOR THE DAIRY-FREE COCONUT
   FROSTING**

8¼ ounces coconut oil

3½ cups powdered sugar

⅓ cup dried unsweetened
   coconut flakes

grated zest of 1 lime

1 Preheat the oven to 350°F. Line two 12-hole muffin pans with 20 cupcake liners (or you can bake in batches).

2 In a large bowl, combine the flour, sugar, baking soda, and cinnamon. In a separate bowl, combine the oil, eggs, and vanilla. Stir into the dry ingredients.

3 Mash the bananas and add them to the batter, along with the pineapple and pecans. Stir with a wooden spoon until just combined.

4 Spoon the batter into the cupcake liners until they are two-thirds full and bake for about 20 minutes until firm to the touch and a knife inserted in the center comes out clean. Remove from the oven and transfer to a wire rack. Let cool in the pan for 5 minutes before turning out and letting cool completely.

5 To make the frosting, place the coconut oil in a bowl and microwave for 30 seconds or until melted. Beat in the powdered sugar in 2 batches until smooth and the right consistency. Stir in the coconut and lime zest to taste.

6 Top the cupcakes with a swirl of coconut frosting and decorate with edible flowers.

Store for 2–3 days in an airtight container at room temperature. Not suitable for freezing.

VARIATION
Alternatively, this batter will make 4 x 8 inch round layers, which can be sandwiched together to make one large layer cake.

Pumpkin Cupcakes with Cream Cheese Frosting and sprinkled with pecan praline.

Pumpkin Cupcakes with Cream Cheese Frosting

MAKES 12 CUPCAKES

1¾ cups self-rising flour

1 teaspoon baking soda

1 teaspoon ground ginger

1 teaspoon ground cinnamon

scant ⅔ cup sunflower oil

scant ⅔ cup sour cream

generous 1 cup soft light brown
sugar

2 large eggs

½ cup canned pumpkin purée

½ cup chopped pecans

1 quantity of Cream Cheese
Frosting (see page 134),
made with the addition of
1 teaspoon ground cinnamon

1 quantity of Praline (see page
134) to decorate, made with
⅓ cup toasted pecans and
½ cup superfine sugar
(optional)

Muffins and cupcakes are a great introduction to baking. With the added benefit of antioxidant rich, fiber rich, naturally sweet pumpkin, these are also a great way to get more vegetables into your diet.

1 Preheat the oven to 400°F. Line a 12-hole muffin or cupcake pan with cupcake liners.

2 Sift together the flour, baking soda, ginger, and cinnamon. In a separate bowl, mix together the oil, sour cream, light brown sugar, eggs, and pumpkin purée. Add the wet ingredients to the dry and stir well. Stir in the pecans.

3 Spoon the muffin batter into the prepared liners until two-thirds full. Bake for 15–20 minutes until well risen and golden brown.

4 Let cool on a wire rack before topping with the cinnamon flavored Cream Cheese Frosting and decorate with Pecan Praline, if using.

Store for 2–3 days in an airtight container in the refrigerator. Suitable for freezing.

TOP TIP
The praline will produce more than is required. Blend one-third of the praline to a fine powder in a food processor and sprinkle it over the frosting. Roughly chop the remainder with a knife and decorate each cupcake.

VARIATION
Substitute the canned pumpkin purée with freshly grated pumpkin.

Friands are small oval tea cakes, originating from France. They are popular as a lighter muffin-style cake, made with ground almonds, egg whites, and powdered sugar. They have less butter and flour and, therefore, fewer calories and less fat than regular muffins. They are surprisingly easy to make and can be flavored with fruits, spices, citrus zest, coconut, nuts, or chocolate. I add blueberries, as the tart acidity of the berries marries beautifully with the sweet cake beneath.

"You've Got a Friand in Me"—Blueberry Friands

MAKES 12 FRIANDS

generous ¾ cup/1¾ sticks
    unsalted butter, melted and
    cooled, plus extra for greasing

1¾ cups powdered sugar

generous ⅓ cup all-purpose flour

2 cups ground almonds

6 medium egg whites (about
    7½ ounces)

grated zest of 1 orange

1¼ cups blueberries

½ cup sliced almonds

1 Preheat the oven to 350°F. Generously grease 12 friand molds or a 12-hole mini muffin pan.

2 Sift the powdered sugar and flour into a bowl. Add the ground almonds and mix well.

3 In a separate bowl, whisk the egg whites to a soft foam. Make a well in the center of the dry ingredients and add the egg whites, orange zest, and melted butter. Stir to form a soft batter.

4 Carefully spoon the batter evenly into the friand molds or mini muffin pan. Place 5 blueberries on top of each friand and sprinkle with almonds.

5 Bake for 20 minutes until firm to the touch, risen, and golden. Let cool in the pan for 5 minutes before carefully turning out onto a wire rack to cool completely. Serve fresh and just warm.

Best eaten fresh on the day they are made.

VARIATION

LEMON & GINGER FRIANDS—omit the blueberries, orange zest, and sliced almonds. Peel and grate a ¾ inch piece of ginger and add to the friand mixture with the zest of 1 lemon and 1 tablespoon poppy seeds. Drizzle with Lemon Syrup (see page 198) and top with 1½ ounces chopped stem ginger in syrup.

LEFT Orange and blueberry friands baked in their distinctive oval pan. Use a mini muffin pan for these, if you don't have a friand pan. RIGHT Lemon, poppy seed, and ginger friands with a delicate lemon syrup.

I have enjoyed making these raspberry jam buns for as long as I have been baking. Comparatively low in butter, compared with other buns, they are flavored with currants and nutmeg. The secret is to shape the bun to create the largest well that will hold the biggest dollop of jam or raspberry fruit spread. Healthier than a donut, but with just as much fun, trying to save the jam mouthful to last! They are great to make with children.

F

MAKES 9 BUNS

Raspberry Jam Buns

1¾ cups self-rising flour

¾ cup whole wheat flour

1 heaping teaspoon ground
    nutmeg

1 teaspoon baking powder

generous ½ cup/1⅛ sticks
    unsalted butter

generous ½ cup soft light brown
    sugar

½ cup currants, soaked in
    4 tablespoons boiling water
    for 1 hour

1 large egg, beaten

3 tablespoons milk

½ a jar seedless raspberry jam

1 Preheat the oven to 350°F. Line a baking sheet with parchment paper.

2 Sift together the flours, nutmeg, and baking powder. Rub the butter into the flour until it resembles fine breadcrumbs, then stir in the sugar and currants. Make a well in the center and add the egg and enough milk to make a stiff but not dry dough.

3 Shape the dough into 9 balls and place them on the baking sheet with a little space between each one. Press a wooden spoon handle into the bun and give it a little wiggle to make a well.

4 Stir the jam until smooth, then place a large teaspoon of jam into the well of each bun.

5 Bake for 20 minutes until golden brown. Let cool for a minute before lifting each bun on to a wire rack to cool.

Store for up to 7 days in an airtight container in a cool, dry place. Not suitable for freezing.

3

4

Chocolate-dusted Orange Madeleines

MAKES 18 MADELEINES

2 eggs

½ cup superfine sugar

½ cup/1 stick melted butter, plus
   extra for greasing

3 tablespoons unsweetened cocoa
   powder, plus extra for dusting

generous ½ cup all-purpose flour

⅓ cup ground almonds

grated zest of 1 orange

¾ teaspoon baking powder

The French madeleine is a delicate genoise cake baked in a distinctive shell mold, and is often made with lemon or orange zest and ground almonds. They are the perfect size to be satisfying with a cup of tea or coffee. They need no additional embellishment and are best eaten on the same day they are made.

1 Whisk the eggs and sugar together in a large bowl until frothy. Fold in the remaining ingredients, then let the mixture stand for about 20 minutes to thicken.

2 Preheat the oven to 400°F. Butter a 12-hole madeleine pan and dust with cocoa powder.

3 Transfer the egg mixture to a pitcher or large pastry bag and carefully fill each mold until three-quarters full (you will need to bake in batches to use all the batter). Bake for 8–10 minutes until golden and risen in the middle. Let cool for 5 minutes before lifting each madeleine out to cool on a wire rack.

VARIATION
Replace the orange zest with lemon zest or vanilla bean paste.

2

3

MUFFINS, CUPCAKES, & MORE

Versatile scones can be enjoyed as a sweet or savory treat. Go back to basics with plain buttermilk scones, add a favorite fruit with berry or lemon and raisin scones, or go savory with pumpkin scones.

Scones are traditionally served with Afternoon Tea, along with clotted cream and strawberry jam. They are just as satisfying, enjoyed with a little butter, with morning coffee or an afternoon cup of tea. They can be easily embellished with spices, such as cinnamon, lemon and ginger, apple and brown sugar, or chocolate, and they are delicious both savory and sweet.

TOP TIP
Stamp out the scones—do not twist them as this will cause the scones to rise unevenly.

Plain Buttermilk Scones

MAKES 6 SCONES

1¾ cups self-rising flour, plus extra for dusting

½ teaspoon salt

1¾ ounces unsalted butter

1¼ ounces superfine sugar

scant ⅔ cup buttermilk

1 egg, beaten, or milk, to glaze

1 Preheat the oven to 425°F. Flour a baking sheet.

2 Sift the flour with the salt in a large bowl. Mix in the butter until the mixture resembles breadcrumbs, then stir in the sugar. Make a deep well in the flour and pour in the buttermilk. Mix to form a soft dough with a knife—do not overwork.

3 Transfer the dough to a lightly floured surface and knead very gently to bring the dough together. Lightly roll or press the dough to a thickness of 1 inch and stamp out 6 rounds with a 2¼-inch pastry cutter.

4 Place the rounds on the floured baking sheet and brush them with a beaten egg or milk to glaze. Bake for 8–10 minutes or until the scones are well risen and brown. Let them cool on a wire rack and serve warm with clotted cream (or crème fraîche) and strawberry jam.

VARIATIONS

BERRY SCONES—make the base mixture as above. Roll the dough to two 6 x 10 inch rectangles. Spread some Berry Compote (see page 19) over one rectangle and place the other rectangle on top. Cut into triangles and place on a baking sheet lined with parchment paper. Brush with milk and sprinkle with demerara sugar. Bake for 20 minutes until golden brown. LEMON & RAISIN SCONES—make as above, but add the grated zest of 1 lemon and 1¼ ounces raisins. Serve with homemade Lemon Curd (see page 18).

2

3

4

Pumpkin Scones

MAKES 6 SCONES

1¾ cups self-rising flour, plus
extra for dusting

1 teaspoon baking powder

1½ ounces unsalted butter

⅔ cup grated Cheddar cheese

1 tablespoon finely chopped
rosemary

scant 1 cup canned pumpkin
purée

⅓ cup milk, plus extra to glaze

1 Preheat the oven to 425°F.
Flour a baking sheet.

2 Sift the flour with the baking
powder in a large bowl.
Combine with the butter
until the mixture resembles
breadcrumbs, then stir in the
cheese and rosemary.

3 Make a deep well in the flour
and add the pumpkin purée,
and just enough milk to make
a soft dough, with a knife—do
not overwork.

4 Turn the dough out onto a
lightly floured surface and

knead very gently to bring the
dough together.

5 Lightly roll or press the dough
to a thickness of 1 inch and
stamp out 6 rounds with a
2¼-inch pastry cutter.

6 Place on the floured baking
sheet and brush with milk to
glaze. Bake for 8–10 minutes
or until well risen and brown.
Let cool on a wire rack and
serve warm with butter.

Best eaten fresh on the day
they are made.

Cookies

Cookies are the perfect accompaniment at any time of the day—and how lovely to bake your own, so you can pack them full of flavor and texture, and not just sugar, fat, and salt. These recipes use ingredients with integrity to tickle your taste buds, satisfy your palate, and show off your baking skills. From super simple nut butter jam cookies to honey nut nougat, I am sure you will find delicious, nutritious, recipes here that will quickly become your favorites.

Anzac Cookies

These rustic cookies, made with rolled oats, are egg free and were originally made by Australian soldiers' wives to send abroad without spoiling. Oats are a valuable source of thiamine (Vitamin B1), iron, and fiber. They contain antioxidants, which can help prevent heart disease, and contain beta-glucan slow-release complex carbohydrate, which may help those with Type-2 diabetes control their blood sugar levels. They are quick and easy to make, and a perfect breakfast on the go for anyone who loves oatmeal.

(F) (EF)

MAKES 18–22 COOKIES

scant 1 cup rolled oats

scant ⅓ cup steel-cut oats

scant 1 cup dried unsweetened
   coconut flakes

¾ cup all-purpose flour

½ cup soft light brown sugar

1 teaspoon ground cinnamon

½ cup/1 stick unsalted butter

1 tablespoon light corn syrup

1 teaspoon baking soda

COOKIES

1 Preheat the oven to 350°F. Line a baking sheet with parchment paper.

2 Place the oats, coconut, flour, sugar, and cinnamon in a bowl and stir.

3 Melt the butter and light corn syrup together in a small pan. Blend the baking soda with 2 tablespoons boiling water and add it to the butter and syrup.

4 Make a well in the dry ingredients and pour in the buttery syrup. Stir until everything is fully incorporated.

5 Place a spoonful of the mixture (each weighing about ¾ ounce) onto the baking sheet, spaced well apart, and bake for 8–10 minutes until golden. These cookies will spread.

6 Remove the cookies from the oven, let cool for 1 minute, then transfer to a wire rack with a metal spatula to cool completely.

Store for up to 21 days in an airtight container at room temperature. Not suitable for freezing.

TOP TIP

Steel-cut oats are the inner kernels of whole groats that have been roughly chopped, offering a chewier texture and nutty flavor.

Nut Butter Jam Cookies

These morsels are packed full of energy, and, as they are homemade, they contain no refined sugar and no added salt. You can make them small enough to be a satisfying bite, as well as portion and calorie controlled! They are fun to make with children and great for beginners.

MAKES 36 COOKIES

⅔ cup/1¼ sticks unsalted butter

¾ cup soft light brown sugar

2 egg yolks

scant ½ cup peanut butter (crunchy, no added salt)— or cashew, almond, or hazelnut butter

1½ cups self-rising flour, plus extra for dusting

7 ounces strawberry jam

1 Preheat the oven to 350°F. Line a baking sheet with parchment paper.

2 Cream the butter and sugar together in a bowl until softened. Add the egg yolks and peanut butter and blend until well mixed. Add the flour and stir to make a soft dough.

3 With lightly floured hands, break off walnut-sized pieces of dough (each weighing about ¾ ounce). Place them on the prepared baking sheet, spaced well apart, and press gently to flatten them slightly.

4 Make a deep well in the center of each flattened ball of dough using the handle of a wooden spoon or your thumb; the cookies will flatten and spread out as they bake.

5 Stir the jam until it is smooth and a little runny, then spoon a teaspoonful into the center of each cookie. Bake on the middle rack of the oven for 10–12 minutes until golden. Transfer to a wire rack to cool.

Store for up to 5 days in an airtight container at room temperature. Not suitable for freezing.

TOP TIPS

Nut Butters and Jams:
- Look for nut butters with no added salt, sugar, or oil.
- Store in a cool dry place to avoid rancidity.
- Look for jams with raw sugar whenever possible.

Chocolate chunk cookies are a staple in many homes —so how can these be made healthier? I have included a higher cocoa solids chocolate, which will reduce the sweetness, but still deliver a real chocolate hit. I have then used hazelnut butter and chopped roasted hazelnuts to add flavor and texture, reducing the overall amount of butter, and have only used light brown sugar to create a chewy cookie. I have also made them slightly smaller—for portion control!

Chocolate Chunk Cookies

MAKES 12 COOKIES

10½ ounces dark chocolate (between 55% and 70% cocoa solids)

⅓ cup/¾ stick unsalted butter

½ cup light brown sugar

scant ½ cup hazelnut butter (crunchy)

1 medium egg

1 teaspoon vanilla extract

¾ cup self-rising flour

generous ¾ cup roughly chopped roasted hazelnuts

1 Preheat the oven to 350°F. Line a baking sheet with parchment paper.

2 Chop 7 ounces of the chocolate into rough chunks. Melt the remaining chocolate in a large heatproof bowl over a pan of simmering water or in the microwave. Let cool slightly.

3 Stir in the butter, sugar, hazelnut butter, egg, and vanilla and beat until smooth. Stir in the flour, chopped hazelnuts, and remaining chocolate chunks. Cover and chill the mixture for 10 minutes.

4 Drop 12 spoonfuls of the mixture onto the prepared baking sheet with plenty of room between each spoonful to allow for spreading.

5 Bake for 10 minutes until very lightly browned. Be careful not to overbake, they should be gently chewy on the inside. Remove from the oven and let cool for 3 minutes before lifting them on to a wire rack with a palette knife to cool completely. Enjoy fresh on the day while still warm!

Store for up to 3 days in an airtight container at room temperature. Not suitable for freezing.

VARIATION
Substitute the hazelnut butter and hazelnuts with almonds, cashews, or peanuts to find your favorite flavor.

COOKIES

Vanilla and Chocolate
Party Rings decorated
with dark chocolate
and colored sprinkles.

Party Rings

MAKES 16–18 PARTY RINGS

generous 1 cup/2¼ sticks
    unsalted butter, softened

½ cup powdered sugar

generous 1¾ cups all-purpose
    flour

½ cup cornstarch

generous ½ cup ground almonds

2 teaspoons vanilla bean paste

2 ounces dark chocolate, melted

sprinkles, to decorate

These soft creamed cookies are egg-free and hand-piped. They have a slightly crumbly texture and literally melt in the mouth, thanks to the inclusion of powdered sugar and cornstarch. The ground almonds add moisture from the natural oils, along with great flavor and texture.

1 Preheat the oven to 350°F. Line a baking sheet with parchment paper.

2 Place all the ingredients, except the chocolate, in a food processor or blender and blend on medium-high speed until well combined and smooth.

3 Fill a large pastry bag with an open star nozzle and the cookie batter. Pipe fingers, rounds, or S-shaped cookies on the prepared baking sheets.

4 Bake the cookies for 12–15 minutes until very lightly browned. Remove from the oven and let cool for 3 minutes before transferring them to a wire rack with a metal spatula to cool completely.

5 Melt the chocolate in a double boiler or microwave oven and fill a pastry bag. Snip the end and drizzle chocolate over the cookies. Decorate with the sprinkles, then let them set.

Store for up to 3 days in an airtight container at room temperature. Not suitable for freezing.

VARIATION
CHOCOLATE PARTY RINGS—replace ½ cup of the all-purpose flour with cocoa powder.

COOKIES

These ginger cookies are classics made with unrefined sugar, molasses, butter, flour, and spices, and with no added salt. They are simple to make, but have such a distinctive flavor and texture they are instantly satisfying —and portion controlled.

Chewy Ginger Cookies

MAKES 16 COOKIES

⅓ cup/¾ stick unsalted butter

½ cup soft light brown sugar

1 medium egg

2 tablespoons molasses

scant 1 cup all-purpose flour

1 teaspoon ground ginger

1 teaspoon ground cinnamon

¼ teaspoon ground cloves

1 teaspoon baking soda

FOR THE LEMON GLAZE

generous ⅓ cup powdered sugar

juice of 1 lemon

1 Preheat the oven to 375°F. Line a baking sheet with parchment paper.

2 Place the butter in a pan to melt, then let cool slightly. Add the sugar, egg, and molasses and beat until smooth.

3 In a separate bowl, sift together the dry ingredients. Beat the dry ingredients into the sugar and butter mixture and stir to form a dough. Wrap the dough in plastic wrap and chill for 2 hours.

4 Pinch off walnut-sized pieces of the dough (each weighing about ¾ ounce) and roll them into balls. Place on the prepared baking sheet about 2 inches apart. Bake for 8–10 minutes until they're browned, spread out, and dry on the surface. Transfer to a wire rack to cool completely.

5 Make the lemon glaze by mixing the powdered sugar with enough lemon juice to make a thin runny icing. Fill a pastry bag and snip the end. Drizzle the icing over the cookies while they are on the rack. Let them set for 30 minutes before serving.

Store for up to 3 days in an airtight container at room temperature. Not suitable for freezing.

These are English-style macaroons, rather than the little French, sandwiched delicacies. Larger, round almond cookies, they are traditionally baked on rice paper circles. They are by nature gluten-free and dairy-free, made with ground almonds and superfine sugar. Adjust the size to make small petits four-style cookies, and enjoy them instead of chocolates. These macaroons are fun to make and package in bags or boxes as gifts.

Almond Macaroons

MAKES 16–18 MACAROONS

2 medium egg whites

1¼ cups ground almonds

generous ¾ cup superfine sugar

16–18 blanched almond halves

TOP TIP

Bake the macaroons on discs of edible rice paper and package in clear bags tied with ribbon.

1 Preheat the oven to 350°F. Line a baking sheet with parchment paper.

2 Whisk the egg whites until foamy. Place the ground almonds in a separate bowl and add one-quarter of the egg whites. Mix, then add half the sugar. Mix again before adding another quarter of the egg whites and the remaining sugar. Add another quarter of the egg whites and mix. The mixture should now be soft enough to shape into 16–18 walnut-sized balls (each weighing ¾ ounce). If it is too stiff, add the remaining egg whites.

3 Place the balls on the prepared baking sheet, spaced well apart. Brush each with a little cold water, then press an almond lightly on the top. Bake for 20 minutes until very lightly browned. Be careful not to overbake, they should be gently chewy on the inside. Transfer to a wire rack to cool.

Store for up to 14 days in an airtight container at room temperature. Not suitable for freezing.

VARIATION

Add 1½ teaspoons freeze-dried raspberry or blackcurrant powder to the ground almonds to flavor the macaroons.

Homemade nougat is deceptively
easy to make, dairy free, and packed
full of roasted nuts and fruits.

Nougat is a dairy-free, gluten-free, honey meringue, packed full of roasted nuts and semi-dried fruits, rolled in a thin slab, and cut into bite-sized treats. It is important to reach the desired temperatures to ensure the eggs are safe to eat and the nougat sets firm, but not too brittle and hard. Your choice of honey will subtly affect the flavor, as will your choice of nuts and fruits.

Nougat

GF DF LF

MAKES 48 BITE-SIZED PIECES

generous 2 cups superfine sugar

3½ ounces corn syrup

⅓ cup water

scant ½ cup orange blossom honey

2 large egg whites

1½ cups sliced almonds, roasted (see page 94)

1 cup whole hazelnuts, roasted

scant ½ cup pistachios, roasted

3 ounces naturally-colored maraschino cherries or dried cherries

generous ½ cup chopped apricots

two 11½ x 16½ inch sheets rice paper

1 Place the sugar (reserving 2 tablespoons) in a saucepan with the corn syrup and just enough water to cover. Melt over medium heat and continue until the temperature reaches 275°F on a candy thermometer. Add the honey and continue to heat to 293°F.

2 Meanwhile, place the egg whites and the reserved sugar in a clean bowl and whisk to the stiff peak stage. With the mixer on medium speed, pour the hot syrup carefully and steadily into the meringue.

3 Once all the syrup has been poured in, continue to mix on full speed for 5 minutes until the meringue has cooled, thickened, and is glossy and lukewarm to touch. Carefully fold the nuts and fruits into the meringue.

4 Lay one sheet of rice paper on a baking sheet and spread the nougat evenly onto the paper. Place the other sheet on top and use a rolling pin to achieve an even finish. Let the meringue cool and firm up overnight.

5 Use a large knife to cut the nougat into bite-sized pieces.

Store for up to 14 days in an airtight container at room temperature. Not suitable for home freezing.

TOP TIP
Crystallized ginger and figs are great alternative ingredients. Also, experiment with different kinds of honey to find your favorite.

1

2

3

3

4

TOP Almond and Cranberry Biscotti.
BOTTOM Chocolate and Pistachio Biscotti
—dairy-free, intensely crunchy cookies.

Biscotti are also known as "cantuccini," and are Italian almond cookies that originated in the city of Prato. They are twice-baked, oblong-shaped, dry, and crunchy. Traditionally, they are dipped in vin santo, but are now often served with coffee and tea. Biscotti are composed exclusively of flour, sugar, eggs, and nuts, including pine nuts, hazelnuts, or almonds that are not roasted or skinned. The traditional recipe uses no yeast or fat—so these cookies are low in calories and dairy-free. The cookie dough is cooked twice, with the second baking defining how hard the biscotti will be.

Almond & Cranberry Biscotti

MAKES 36–40 BISCOTTI

generous 1¾ cups all-purpose flour, plus extra for dusting

1 cup superfine sugar

2 teaspoons baking powder

2 large eggs

generous 1 cup dried cranberries

generous 1 cup whole almonds

grated zest of 1 orange (or 3 drops of orange oil)

powdered sugar, for dusting

1 Preheat the oven to 375°C. Line a baking sheet with parchment paper.

2 Mix the flour, sugar, and baking powder in a bowl. Add the eggs and whisk until the mix resembles a crumble topping. Add the cranberries, almonds, and orange and stir to form a soft dough, taking care not to overmix at this stage. The dough should be gently crumbly but not tough.

3 Turn the dough out onto a lightly floured surface and divide it into three pieces. Carefully roll each piece into a log about 1¼ inches wide and place them apart on the prepared baking sheet. Bake for 20 minutes until they are lightly browned and firm to the touch.

4 Remove the baking sheet from the oven and turn the oven down to 120°F. Let the logs cool on the baking sheet, dusting them with powdered sugar while they are still warm.

5 Using a sharp serrated knife, cut the logs into ¾-inch wide slices, and place the pieces back on the baking sheet, allowing space between each one for the air to circulate. Bake for 1 hour, until they have dried out, and are slightly brittle.

Store for up to 7 days in an airtight container at room temperature. Not suitable for freezing.

These biscotti combine chocolate and pistachios, which you can happily dunk into your morning cappuccino, offering a dairy-free, lower fat, reduced calorie, deliciously crunchy cookie. You're welcome!

Chocolate & Pistachio Biscotti

MAKES 20–24 BISCOTTI

1 large egg

generous ½ cup superfine sugar

generous ¾ cup all-purpose flour

2 tablespoons unsweetened cocoa powder

generous 1 cup pistachios, shelled

3½ ounces dairy-free dark chocolate chips (70% cocoa solids)—or a bar of dairy-free chocolate, grated

1 Preheat the oven to 375°F. Line a baking sheet with parchment paper.

2 Whisk the egg and sugar in a large bowl until the texture is light and fluffy.

3 Stir in the flour and cocoa powder, then add the pistachios and chocolate chips. The dough should be quite sticky at this stage. Flour your hands and divide the dough into 2 portions

4 Shape each portion into a log about 1¼ inches wide and place them on the prepared baking sheet. Bake the logs in the oven for about 20 minutes until they're firm to the touch with a good crust.

5 Remove the baking sheet from the oven, transfer it to a wire rack and let it cool. Reduce the oven temperature to 120°F.

6 Using a sharp serrated knife, cut the logs into ¾-inch wide slices, and place the pieces back on the baking tray, allowing space between each one, so that the air can circulate. Bake for 1 hour until they have dried out and are slightly brittle.

Store for up to 7 days in an airtight container at room temperature. Not suitable for freezing.

4

6

6

COOKIES

Homemade decorated cookies are a wonderful gift and fun to make. I have used white royal icing for an authentic decoration. This dough can be used to create cookies for every occasion, from baby showers to birthdays, Halloween to Thanksgiving. For added sparkle, finish the cookies with an edible pearl luster dust.

Snowflake Vanilla Cookies

ICING TOP TIPS

- Look for cartons of lightly pasteurized egg whites available in the refrigerated section of the grocery store. These are safe, have up to 1 month's shelf life, unopened, and a 7-day shelf life, once opened, and kept refrigerated. The cartons can also be frozen and defrosted for use as required.
- The added lemon juice strengthens the icing and imparts a subtle flavor.
- Once you have made the royal icing, if it looks grainy or really stiff, add a little more egg white and continue to whisk for 2 minutes on high speed.
- Royal icing once made, will keep in an airtight container for up to 7 days. Re-whisk daily before use.

TOP TIP

Use a straw to make a small hole in the cookie before you bake them so that you can hang them from a ribbon.

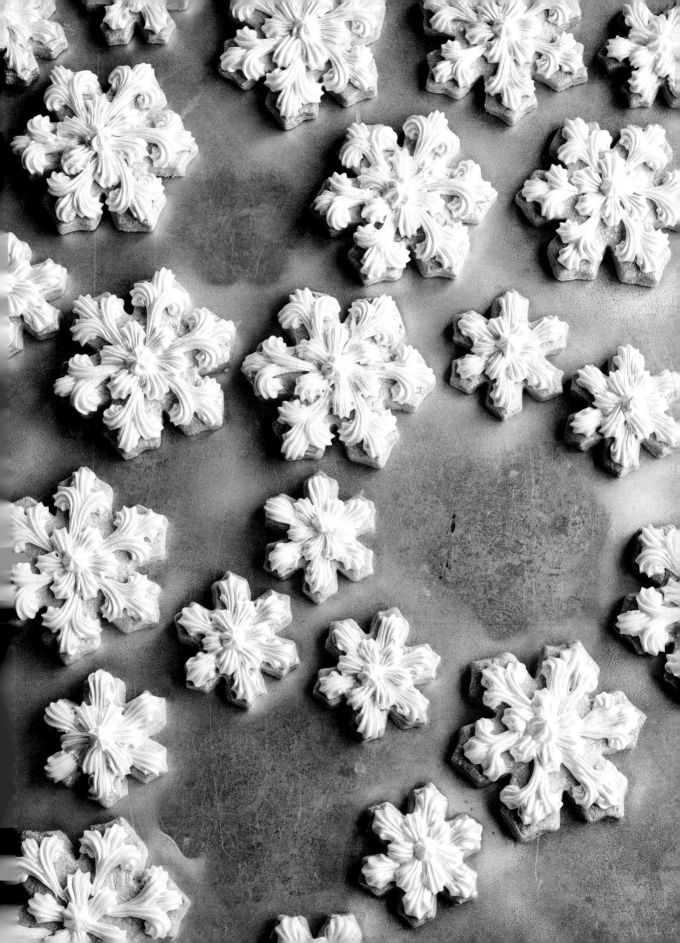

Snowflake Vanilla Cookies

**MAKES 24–30 COOKIES
DEPENDING ON THE SIZE**

generous ¾ cup/1¾ sticks
    unsalted butter, softened

1 cup superfine sugar

1 medium egg, beaten

3 cups all-purpose flour, plus
    extra for dusting

1 teaspoon baking powder

1 teaspoon vanilla powder or
    2 teaspoons vanilla bean paste

FOR THE ROYAL ICING

5 ounces egg whites, at room
    temperature

4¼–5⅓ cups powdered sugar

juice of 1 lemon

1 Cream the butter and sugar together, then add the beaten egg and mix to combine. Gently fold in the flour, baking powder, and vanilla powder, and mix until a dough forms. Wrap the dough in plastic wrap and chill for 30 minutes.

2 Preheat the oven to 350°F. Line a baking sheet with parchment paper. Lightly flour the counter and roll the dough to a thickness of ¼–½ inch. Stamp out snowflake cookie shapes and place on the prepared baking sheet, spaced well apart. Bake for 10–12 minutes until pale golden, then transfer to a wire rack to cool.

3 To make the icing, whisk the egg whites in a bowl until they're soft and foamy. Add the powdered sugar. Mix on super slow speed until the sugar is incorporated, then on high speed until the icing is glossy, and has the consistency of freshly whipped heavy cream. Pour the lemon juice through a tea strainer into the bowl and continue to whisk for 2 minutes. The icing should be glossy and thick but not overstiff or dry.

4 To decorate, fill the pastry bags with the icing and use plain or star tips to hand-pipe the cookies. Alternatively, use ready-made tubes of colored icings and gels.

Store for up to 28 days in an airtight container at room temperature. Not suitable for freezing.

4

Gingerbread cookies are wonderful to decorate for the holidays, as simple or as intricate as you like. You don't need to invest in a huge amount of money, time, or skill to achieve a fabulous result that will also build your confidence in sugar decoration. These spiced cookies are perfect for Halloween, Thanksgiving, and Christmas. Use your own cookie cutters to create decorations, gifts, or birthday treats instead of the wreath.

Gingerbread Wreath

MAKES 24–30 COOKIES DEPENDING ON THE SIZE

3¼ cups all-purpose flour, plus extra for dusting

1 tablespoon ground ginger

2 teaspoons ground cinnamon

½ teaspoon ground nutmeg

¼ teaspoon ground cloves

1 level teaspoon baking powder

½ teaspoon baking soda

1 teaspoon vanilla powder (or 2 teaspoons vanilla extract)

generous 1 cup unsalted butter, softened

generous ¾ cup muscovado (dark brown) sugar

1 large egg yolk

5¾ ounces molasses

1–2 tablespoons milk

TO DECORATE

1 quantity of Royal Icing (see page 86)

green and red food coloring gels

red sugar pearls

1 Preheat the oven to 350°F. Line a baking sheet with parchment paper.

2 In a mixing bowl, sift together the flour, spices, baking powder and baking soda—and add the vanilla powder, if using.

3 Cream the butter and sugar together in a bowl. Blend the egg yolk together with the molasses and milk. Add the vanilla extract here, if using. Whisk into the creamed mixture. Add the flour to the batter and mix until the dough just comes together. Wrap the dough in plastic wrap and chill for 30 minutes.

4 Lightly knead the dough and roll it out on a lightly floured counter. Use a 6-inch and 10-inch round pan to cut out a ring of dough for the base of the wreath from the rolled out dough, then carefully place it on the prepared sheet.

5 Use a 2¼-inch and 3¼-inch holly cookie cutter to cut out 36 holly cookies and place them on the prepared baking sheets (or bake in batches if necessary).

6 Draw a bow on a card, cut it out, and use it as a template to make the bow (or use a bow cookie cutter). Bake the holly cookies for 8 minutes, the bow for 10 minutes, and the wreath for 12–15 minutes until firm and golden. Let them cool on the tray, then transfer to a wire rack.

7 Separate the royal icing into 4 bowls and color them 2 shades of green, a red, and leave one white. To ice the wreath, fill 2 pastry bags with a no. 2 tip and 1 tablespoon of the green icing in separate bags. Pipe outlines on the holly cookies. Thin the remaining green icing with water and spoon it into a pastry bag. Snip the end and fill in the cookies, using a paintbrush to push the icing up to the piped line. Let the cookies set for 1 hour, then pipe over the icing to create texture and design.

Continued overleaf...

TOP TIP

Bake your favorite cookies and decorate with ready-made icing and sprinkles.

8 For the bow, pipe the outline in red with a no. 2 tip and fill it in with thinned red icing. Fill a pastry bag with a no. 3 tip and slightly thinned white icing. Pipe polka dots on the red icing while it is still wet, then let all the iced components set overnight.

9 To assemble, start by fixing the bow in position on the wreath base with stiff white royal icing. Fix the holly pieces in place using white royal icing to secure them. Finish with red sugar pearls iced into position with white royal icing. Let set for 2 hours.

Store for up to 28 days in an airtight container at room temperature. Not suitable for freezing.

7

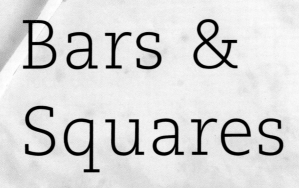

Bars & Squares

Bars are quick and easy to make and bake, and can be a staple for packed lunches, morning coffee, or afternoon snacks. I have adjusted these recipes so they can all be baked in the same size pan— offering you the flexibility to choose a different recipe each week. From simple flapjacks and shortbreads to layered bars and brownies, these treats will build your confidence in baking as well as your repertoire.

MAKES 16 BARS

1 cup/2 sticks unsalted butter
(or vegan margarine or spread
for a dairy-free alternative)

scant 1 cup honey

½ cup soft light brown sugar

3¾ cups rolled oats

½ cup sliced almonds

½ cup golden raisins

½ cup dried apricots

generous ½ cup chopped prunes

¾ cup chopped pitted dates

2 teaspoons fennel seeds

2 teaspoons chia seeds

2 tablespoons pumpkin seeds

2 tablespoons flaxseed

Packed with energy-giving, mineral-rich fruits, seeds, nuts, and oats, these little pocket rockets will keep you fueled all day and satisfy any cravings.

Date, Seed, & Honey Power Bars

1 Preheat the oven to 325°F. Line the bottom and sides of a 12 x 8-inch pan with parchment paper.

2 Melt the butter and honey together. Toss all the dry ingredients together, then pour over the melted butter and honey. Stir to combine.

3 Transfer to the prepared pan, press down, and bake for 40 minutes until golden. Let cool, then chill well before cutting into 16 bars.

Store for up to 7 days in an airtight container in the refrigerator. Not suitable for freezing.

Iron Bars

MAKES 16 BARS

1 cup/2 sticks unsalted butter
(or vegan margarine or spread
for a dairy-free alternative)

scant 1 cup honey

½ cup soft light brown sugar

3¾ cups rolled oats

generous ½ cup cashews, roughly
chopped

½ cup sunflower seeds

1½ cups chopped organic ready-
to-eat dried apricots

A healthy boost of iron will improve the condition of your skin, hair, and nails as well as provide energy, warmth, and vitality. Apricots, cashews, and sunflower seeds are naturally rich sources of iron—enjoy these iron-rich bars with a glass of orange juice, high in vitamin C, for maximum absorption.

1 Preheat the oven to 300°F. Line the bottom and sides of a 12 x 8-inch pan with parchment paper. Melt the butter and honey together. Toss all the dry ingredients together, then pour over the melted butter and honey. Stir to combine.

2 Transfer to the prepared pan, press down, and bake for 40 minutes until golden. Let cool, then chill well before cutting into 16 bars.

Store for up to 7 days in an airtight container in the refrigerator. Not suitable for freezing.

These squares are deliciously nutty and satisfyingly sweet. I like to serve them as an alternative to dessert, with coffee after a meal. They deliver such a hit of flavor, crunch, and sweetness, one small square is the perfect controlled portion.

Almond Toscaner

MAKES 24 SQUARES

½ cup/1 stick unsalted butter, room temperature

scant 1 cup superfine sugar

scant 2 cups ground almonds

8½ ounces whole eggs (about 4 large eggs)

generous ⅓ cup all-purpose flour

1 teaspoon almond extract

FOR THE TOPPING

½ cup/1 stick unsalted butter

½ cup superfine sugar

3½ ounces corn syrup

scant ¼ cup milk

scant 2 cups sliced almonds, toasted (see Tip below)

1 Preheat the oven to 375F. Line the bottom and sides of a 12 x 8-inch pan with parchment paper. Beat the butter, sugar, and almonds together in a bowl. Add the eggs slowly, then fold in the flour. Transfer to the prepared pan and bake for 16–18 minutes.

2 Meanwhile, make the topping. Put the butter, sugar, corn syrup, and milk in a pan, bring to a boil, then simmer for 1–2 minutes, stirring. Remove from the heat and stir in the toasted almonds.

3 Once the bottom of the squares have baked, remove the toscaner from the oven and turn the oven temperature up to 400°F. Spread the topping over the cake, return to the oven, and bake for 6–8 minutes until golden. Let cool completely in the pan, then cut into 24 squares.

Store for 2–3 days in an airtight container at room temperature. Best eaten on the day they are made—the topping will soften and become more chewy with keeping, but this does not deter from the flavor!

VARIATION
Add the grated zest of 1 orange to the almond base before baking, and 1 tablespoon apricot jam to the topping.

TOP TIP

To toast nuts: preheat the oven to 300°F. Spread the nuts out on a baking sheet and bake for 15 minutes until just turning golden.

5

Chocolate and coconut have a wonderful affinity, and these bars combine the best of both ingredients—with a chocolate coconut shortbread topped with an intense, rich dark chocolate ganache. I have used raw sugar and whole wheat flour for added nutrition.

Chocolate Coconut Shortbread

MAKES 16 SQUARES

1⅓cups/2¾ sticks unsalted butter, melted

scant ½ cup cocoa powder

2¼ cups whole wheat flour

generous 1 cup soft light brown sugar

3 teaspoons baking powder

generous 2 cups dried unsweetened coconut

FOR THE CHOCOLATE GANACHE

⅔ cup heavy cream

5½ ounces dark chocolate (between 55 and 70% cocoa solids), broken into pieces

1 Preheat the oven 375°F. Line the bottom and sides of a 12 x 8-inch pan with parchment paper.

2 Melt the butter in a large saucepan and stir in the cocoa. Remove from the heat and stir in all the remaining ingredients. Transfer to the prepared pan and press down. Bake for 25–30 minutes, until risen, firm, and coming away from the sides of the pan.

3 Remove from the oven, transfer to a wire rack, and let cool in the pan for 5 minutes.

4 To make the ganache, bring the cream to a boil in a saucepan, remove from the heat, and stir in the broken chocolate. Stir until melted and smooth.

5 Top the shortbread with the chocolate ganache, let set, then cut into 16 squares.

Store for up to 7 days in an airtight container at room temperature or chilled. Not suitable for freezing.

Date & Apple Squares

MAKES 16 SQUARES

12 ounces cooking apples, peeled, cored and chopped

grated zest and juice of 1 lemon

2 teaspoons ground cinnamon

2½ cups Medjool dates, pitted

¾ cup soft light brown sugar

2¼ cups all-purpose flour

2¼ cups rolled oats

generous 1 cup/2¼ sticks unsalted butter, melted

These bars are nutritious with oats, apple, and dates that are rich in complex carbohydrates, vitamins, minerals, and fiber. The bars are naturally sweet, so I have reduced the overall sugar in this delicious, oaty treat.

1 Preheat the oven to 350°F. Line the bottom and sides of a 12 x 8-inch pan with parchment paper.

2 Place the apple in a saucepan with the lemon zest and juice, and the cinnamon. Bring to a boil and simmer over a low heat for 5 minutes until tender.

3 Add the dates and ¼ cup of the sugar and cook for a further 5 minutes until the mixture is a stiff paste, but not dry. Be careful not to let the mixture boil dry. Add 2–3 tablespoons water if this is looking likely. Remove from the heat.

4 Put the flour, remaining sugar, and oats into a bowl and mix together. Make a well in the center and pour in the melted butter. Mix together to form an oaty, crumbly mixture.

5 Press half the oat mixture into the bottom of the pan and press down firmly. Spread the apple and date mixture over the oaty base, then top with the remaining oat mixture. Press down firmly.

6 Bake for 35 minutes until golden. Let cool in the pan, then cut into 16 squares.

Store for up to 5 days in an airtight container at room temperature or chilled. Not suitable for freezing.

MAKES 16 SQUARES

¾ cup/1½ sticks unsalted butter

¾ cup superfine sugar

generous 1 cup self-rising flour

1 teaspoon baking powder

1 cup ground almonds

3 large eggs

2 teaspoons vanilla extract

⅔ cup sour cream

FOR THE CRUMBLE TOPPING

1½ tablespoon unsalted butter, melted

⅓ cup all-purpose flour, sifted

2½ tablespoons superfine sugar

½ ounce hazelnuts, chopped

1 tablespoon rolled oats

1 tablespoon honey

½ teaspoon ground ginger

FOR THE RHUBARB

14 ounces untrimmed rhubarb

¼ cup soft light brown sugar

grated zest of 1 orange

4

Rhubarb has only 21 calories per 3½ ounces, with no fat and no cholesterol. Rich in glycosides, rhubarb has long been used as a natural laxative. Rhubarb can be "forced," a practice of growing rhubarb in a dark, indoor environment, in order to produce a brighter red, more tender, sweeter-tasting rhubarb than rhubarb grown outdoors. These bars combine rhubarb with vanilla and sour cream in this soft crumble cake.

Rhubarb & Sour Cream Squares

1 Start by making the crumble topping. Combine the butter with the flour and stir in the sugar. Add the chopped hazelnuts, oats, honey, and ginger, then set aside.

2 Next, prepare the rhubarb. Preheat the oven to 400°F. Wipe the rhubarb stalks clean, trim, and discard the ends. Cut the remainder into 1-inch pieces and lay on a roasting tray. Sprinkle with the sugar and orange zest. Cover with foil and roast for 15 minutes. Uncover and roast for a further 5 minutes, then let cool. Drain off all the juices (you can serve them on the side, thickened with a little instant vanilla pudding mix or with powdered sugar to make an icing to drizzle over the top if liked).

3 Reduce the oven to 325°F. Line the bottom and sides of a 12 x 8-inch pan with parchment paper.

4 For the cake, cream the butter and sugar together. Mix the flour with the baking powder and add to the creamed mixture. Add the almonds, eggs, vanilla, and sour cream and beat to make a batter. Spread the cake batter in the bottom of the pan, scatter over the rhubarb, then the crumble topping. Bake for 40–45 minutes until golden and a knife inserted comes out clean. Remove from the oven, transfer to a wire rack and let cool in the pan for 10 minutes before cutting into 16 squares. Serve with whipped cream, if you like.

Store for 1–2 days in an airtight container in the refrigerator. Not suitable for freezing.

LEFT Quick Chocolate
Brownies, packed with fruit
and nuts, are completely
crave-worthy.
RIGHT Salted Caramel
Pumpkin Brownies—for a
truly indulgent treat.

Quick Chocolate Brownies

MAKES 16 BROWNIES

⅔ cup/1¼ sticks unsalted butter or non-dairy substitute

2¾ ounces dark chocolate (70% cocoa solids), broken into pieces

2 teaspoons cocoa powder

generous 1 cup toasted mixed nuts (hazelnuts, pistachios, peanuts, pecans, cashews, almonds), roughly chopped (see page 94 for how to toast nuts)

⅓ cup mixed dried fruits (cherries, cranberries, golden raisins)

3 large eggs

1½ cups soft light brown sugar

½ cup all-purpose flour

1 heaped teaspoon baking powder

These brownies are packed full of dried fruits and roasted nuts to add flavor, texture, and added vitamins and minerals. These brownies contain no refined sugar and no salt. Quick and easy to make, they are perfect for building your confidence.

1 Preheat the oven to 325°F. Line the bottom and sides of a 12 x 8-inch pan with parchment paper.

2 Melt the butter and chocolate together in a heatproof bowl set over a saucepan of simmering water. Remove from the heat and stir in the cocoa. Stir in all the remaining ingredients. Transfer to the prepared pan and press down. Bake for 25–30 minutes until just set.

3 Remove from the oven, transfer to a wire rack, and let cool in the pan, before cutting into 16 brownies.

Store for up to 7 days in an airtight container at room temperature or chilled. Suitable for freezing.

VARIATION

Replace the nuts and fruit with 1½ cups raspberries folded through the batter before baking or add the grated zest of 2 fresh oranges to the brownie batter before baking.

Pumpkin is an excellent source of beta-carotene—which is converted to vitamin A in the body, and is a protective antioxidant. These brownies are delicious throughout the year (with or without the optional caramel), and perfect as a Thanksgiving treat with the addition of salted caramel.

Salted Caramel Pumpkin Brownies

MAKES 15 BROWNIES

1 quantity of Salted Caramel (see page 106) (optional)

1 cup/2 sticks unsalted butter

10½ ounces dark chocolate (55% cocoa solids), broken into pieces

⅔ cup freshly brewed strong coffee

generous ¾ cup soft light brown sugar

generous ¾ cup superfine sugar

2 teaspoons vanilla extract

4 large eggs

generous 1 cup all-purpose flour

FOR THE PUMPKIN FILLING

½ cup cream cheese, room temperature

½ cup canned pumpkin puree

1 egg

¼ cup superfine sugar

1 teaspoon ground cinnamon

½ teaspoon ground ginger

¼ cup all-purpose flour

1 Preheat the oven to 325F. Line the bottom and sides of a 12 x 8-inch pan with parchment paper.

2 If using, make the Salted Caramel sauce, following the instructions on page 106, and spoon the caramel into a pastry bag.

3 Now, make the pumpkin filling. Beat the cream cheese until smooth. Add the pumpkin puree and egg and continue mixing until smooth. Add the sugar, cinnamon, ginger, and flour and mix until well combined and smooth. Set aside.

4 Finally, make the brownie batter. Melt together the butter and chocolate in a heatproof bowl (either in a microwave or over a pan of simmering water). Stir in the coffee and let cool slightly. Stir in the sugars and vanilla and whisk in the eggs. Finally, fold in the flour until well combined and smooth.

5 Pour half the brownie batter into the prepared pan. Spoon two-thirds of the pumpkin mixture over the brownie batter. Pipe half of the Salted Caramel, if using, over the pumpkin. Spoon the remaining brownie batter on top, followed by the pumpkin batter, and finally the Caramel, if using. Use a knife to gently swirl the mixtures together.

6 Bake for 35–40 minutes until the top is set, the edges are coming away from the pan, and a knife inserted should come away moist, but not wet. Remove from the oven, transfer to a wire rack, and let cool in the pan, before cutting into 15 brownies.

Store for up to 7 days in an airtight container at room temperature or chilled. Suitable for freezing.

FOR THE SALTED CARAMEL
SAUCE (OPTIONAL)

⅔ cup heavy cream

¾ cup superfine sugar

1½ tablespoons unsalted butter

a pinch of salt

Put the cream in a saucepan and bring to a boil. Remove from the heat and let cool slightly. Melt and cook the sugar in a saucepan, with no stirring, until it turns a dark caramel color. Remove from the heat and add the cream—a little at first, as it will bubble up, then pour in the remainder. Add the butter and stir until it has melted. Add salt to taste. Cool and let thicken. Store for up to 14 days in a jar in the refrigerator.

SALTED CARAMEL PUMPKIN BROWNIES

5

6

These dairy-free flapjacks can be made with any type of nut butter to add flavor, texture, and nutrition, without a lot of fat and refined sugar. They-re gluten-free, too.

Skinny Peanut Butter Flapjacks

MAKES 16 FLAPJACKS

1⅓ cups Medjool dates, pitted

⅔ cup water

1 cup crunchy peanut butter (or other nut butter, such as cashew, hazelnut, or almond)

3 large egg whites

⅔ cup honey

6½ cups rolled oats (gluten free)

1 Place the dates in a saucepan with the water and simmer until softened and the water has been absorbed. Set aside.

2 Preheat the oven to 325°F. Line a 12 x 8-inch pan with parchment paper.

3 Blend the dates, peanut butter, egg whites, and honey together in a food processor or blender until smooth. Stir in the oats until they are well coated.

4 Transfer the mixture to the prepared pan and press down firmly. Bake for about 30 minutes until golden. Let cool in the pan, then cut into 16 triangles.

Store for up to 5 days in an airtight container at room temperature. Not suitable for freezing.

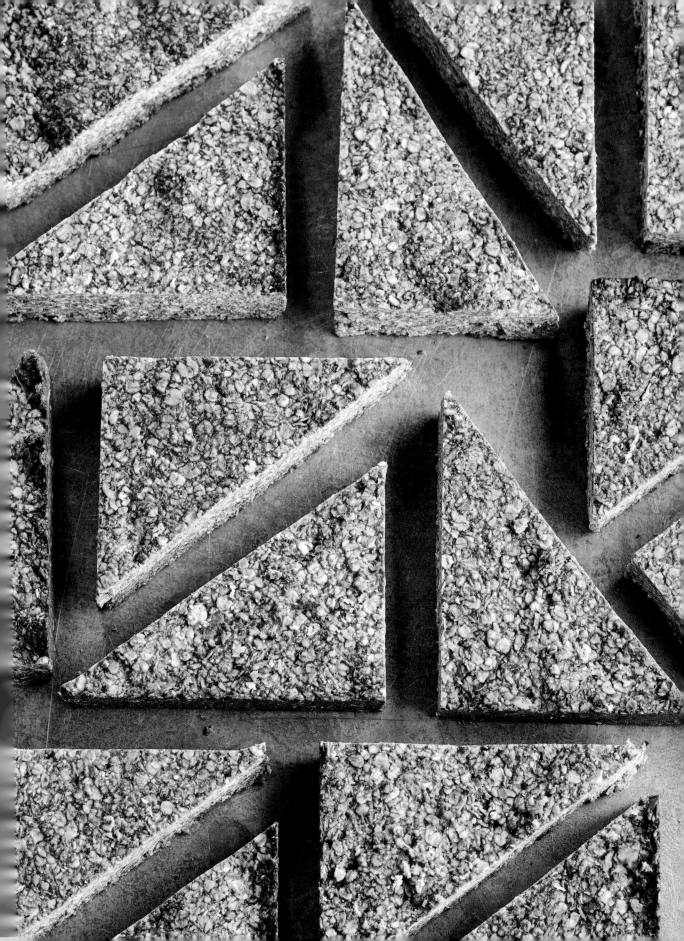

These blondies are made with prunes, which are rich in iron and fiber, and add a wonderful natural sweetness to the mix. I have added a boost of iron and other vitamins, minerals, flavors, and textures with cashew butter and cashews. The sweetness of white chocolate is an extra indulgence.

Prune & Cashew Blondies

MAKES 16 BLONDIES

generous 1 cup/2¼ sticks
    unsalted butter

1¾ cups ready-to-eat prunes,
    pitted and finely chopped

¾ cup superfine sugar

10½ ounces white chocolate,
    broken into pieces

4 medium eggs, beaten

scant 2½ cups all-purpose flour

scant ½ cup cashew butter

generous ¾ cup chopped cashews

1 Preheat the oven to 350°F. Line a 12 x 8-inch pan with parchment paper.

2 Melt the butter, prunes, and sugar in a heavy-based saucepan. Remove from the heat and add the white chocolate, whisking well. Let cool for 10 minutes. Don't be concerned if the mixture looks split at this stage—once the eggs are added, they will help emulsify the batter.

3 Add the beaten eggs and use a balloon whisk to bring everything together into a smooth batter. Add the flour and mix well. Transfer the batter to the prepared pan and level it with the back of a spoon.

4 Drop teaspoons of the cashew butter over the blondie base and marble with a knife. Scatter the surface with roughly chopped cashews. Bake for 25–30 minutes until the blondie is baked, golden brown, and has a slight wobble.

5 Remove from the oven. Let cool on a wire rack. Refrigerate overnight to firm before trimming and cutting into 16 bars.

Store for up to 5 days in an airtight container in the refrigerator. Not suitable for freezing.

VARIATION
Replace the cashew butter and cashews with almond or hazelnut butter and sprinkle with pistachios, pecans, or hazelnuts—experiment to find your favorite.

LEFT Banana Granola Flapjacks
with apricots and hazelnuts.
RIGHT Strawberry and Walnut
Flapjacks.

Banana Granola Flapjacks

MAKES 24 FLAPJACKS

generous ¾ cup/1¾ sticks
    unsalted butter

4 tablespoons honey

scant ½ cup soft light brown
    sugar

3 medium ripe bananas

1 large egg

2¾ cups rolled oats

1 cup self-rising flour

generous ½ cup chopped dried
    apricots

½ cup chopped toasted hazelnuts

These granola bars are loaded with nutritious goodies, including bananas, apricots, and hazelnuts. They provide essential minerals and fiber, and are packed with oats, which will keep you full for longer.

1 Preheat the oven to 325°F. Line a 12 x 8-inch pan with parchment paper.

2 Melt the butter, honey, and sugar together, then let cool. In a separate bowl, mash the bananas with the egg, then stir these into the melted butter and sugar.

3 In a separate bowl, mix the remaining ingredients together.

4 Stir the melted ingredients into the oat mixture and mix until well combined. Transfer to the prepared pan and press down firmly.

5 Bake for 30 minutes until golden. Let cool in the pan, then cut into 24 squares.

Store for up to 5 days at room temperature in an airtight container. Not suitable for freezing.

Flapjack bars are quick and simple to make. Packed with oats and rich in fiber, vitamins, and slow-release carbohydrates, they make an ideal mid-morning snack. I have included walnuts for extra flavor, texture, protein, and essential oils. You can make them gluten-free, too.

Strawberry & Walnut Flapjacks

 EF GF F

MAKES 24 FLAPJACKS

generous ¾ cup/1¾ sticks
   unsalted butter

scant 1 cup soft light brown sugar

¼ cup light corn syrup

¼ cup honey

5½ cups rolled oats
   (gluten-free oats)

1 cup chopped walnuts

18 ounces strawberry, raspberry
   or mixed berry jam

1 Preheat the oven to 325°F. Line a 12 x 8-inch pan with parchment paper.

2 Melt the butter, sugar, syrup, and honey together. Stir in the oats and chopped walnuts.

3 Transfer half the mixture to the prepared pan, press down, and spread with the jam. Top with the remaining flapjack mixture and spread with the remaining jam.

4 Bake for 40 minutes until golden. Let cool in the pan, then cut into 24 squares.

Store for up to 7 days in an airtight container at room temperature. Not suitable for freezing.

VARIATION
Substitute the walnuts with chopped crystallized ginger, chocolate chips, desiccated coconut, or 3 tablespoons peanut, cashew, almond, or hazelnut butter.

I have packed these oat bars with dried fruits and nuts and used coconut oil and honey to bind and sweeten them. Dairy-free, gluten-free, and with no refined sugar—these bars deliver a satisfying and nutritious hit.

"Who Gives a Fig" Bars

MAKES 16 BARS

1½ cups ready-to-eat figs, roughly chopped, with the stems removed

1 cup water

1 tablespoon vanilla bean paste

4½ ounces coconut oil

⅔ cup honey

5 cups rolled oats (gluten-free)

½ cup golden raisins

½ cup dried cherries, cranberries, or goji berries

generous ¾ cup chopped dried apricots

1 cup mixed chopped nuts (hazelnuts, cashews, or almonds)

½ cup dried unsweetened coconut

1 Preheat the oven to 325°F. Line a 12 x 8-inch pan with parchment paper.

2 Place the figs in a pan with the water and the vanilla bean paste. Gently stew the figs for about 10 minutes until softened. Let them cool and absorb the liquid, then blend in a blender to make a paste.

3 In a large saucepan, melt the coconut oil and honey together over low heat, then stir in the fig paste.

4 Place the remaining ingredients together in a bowl and mix well. Stir the fig batter into the dry ingredients and mix until everything is combined. Transfer the mixture to the prepared pan and press down firmly.

5 Bake for 30 minutes until golden. Let cool in the pan, then chill well before cutting into 16 bars.

Store for up to 5 days in an airtight container at room temperature or chilled. Not suitable for freezing.

How often do you head to the movies and mindlessly munch your way through a huge bucket of sweet 'n' salty popcorn? Next time, make these bars ahead of the movies—get the children to join in. They are portion controlled and sweet with added crunch and flavor, thanks to the coconut, peanuts, raisins, and dark chocolate. Better still, they are gluten-free and have no added salt.

"Night at The Movies" Popcorn Bar

MAKES 16 BARS

2 tablespoons sunflower oil

scant ½ cup popping corn

10½ ounces dark chocolate
(55–70% cocoa solids), broken
into pieces

⅓ cup/¾ stick unsalted butter

⅓ cup light corn syrup

⅔ cup dried unsweetened
coconut

generous 1 cup roasted peanuts
(or sunflower seeds)

generous 1 cup raisins

1 Line a 12 x 8-inch pan with parchment paper.

2 Heat the oil in a large saucepan. When the oil is hot, stir in the popping corn. Cover with a tight-fitting lid and cook over low heat, shaking the pan intermittently, until all the kernels have popped.

3 Meanwhile, melt the chocolate, butter, and light corn syrup together in a microwave or a heatproof bowl set over a pan of hot water.

4 Toss the popcorn, coconut, nuts, and raisins with the chocolate and pour into the prepared pan. Press down firmly and chill for about 4–6 hours until set. Turn out of the pan and use a sharp knife to chop into 16 bars.

Store for up to 3 days in an airtight container at room temperature or chilled. Not suitable for freezing.

These oat slices have been a stalwart throughout the years —we always have a batch available—for just when you are looking for a little something. They're enormously satisfying for breakfast, morning coffee, or with an afternoon cup of tea—even a glass of milk before bed! Try adding sunflower seeds, flaxseed, cinnamon, chopped cashews, or almonds to the oat base to find your personal favorite. And they're high in fiber too, with oats and iron-rich fruits, nuts, and seeds.

Oaty Date Slices

MAKES 16 SLICES

generous 1¾ cups all-purpose flour

generous ¾ cup whole wheat flour

generous ½ cup soft light brown
    sugar

scant 2 cups rolled oats

generous 1 cup/2¼ sticks
    unsalted butter, melted

3 cups Medjool dates, pitted and
    roughly chopped

grated zest of 2 lemons

⅔ cup water

VARIATION

Substitute the dates for unsulfured apricots—these have a wonderful caramelized flavor—and add a scant ½ cup sunflower seeds and a scant ½ cup chopped cashews to the oat base, for a boost of fiber and iron.

1 Preheat the oven to 350°F. Line the bottom and sides of a 12 x 8-inch pan with parchment paper.

2 Measure the flours, sugar, and oats into a bowl and mix. Make a well in the center and pour in the melted butter. Mix together to form an oaty, crumbly mixture.

3 Put the dates in a saucepan with the lemon zest and water. Heat over medium-high heat until the dates have softened and the water has been absorbed. Press half the oat mixture into the bottom of the pan and press down firmly. Spread the date mixture over the base, then top with the remaining oat mixture. Press down firmly.

4 Bake for 35–40 minutes until golden. Remove from the oven. Let cool in the pan, then cut into 16 slices.

Store for up to 5 days in an airtight container at room temperature or chilled. Not suitable for freezing.

TOP TIP

Dried apricots are treated with sulfur dioxide to retain their orange coloring, which destroys the vitamin B1 content. Look instead for unsulfured or organic apricots—these will be darker brown in color, as they have been naturally dried. They will be more caramelized and sweeter in flavor, with a less pronounced sharp, tangy flavor, and will retain their vitamin B1 content (the packages are usually sealed so as not to show their supposedly less desirable darker brown color).

"The Power of Three"

Is it a cookie? Is it a brownie? Is it a coconut macaroon? It's all three! The perfect choice when your willpower needs a helping hand—rather than three separate treats, you get to have all three in one! These bite-sized squares are a huge hit with our clientele in The Middle East. Wonderfully sweet and decadent with layers of peanut butter cookie, chocolate brownie, and coconut macaroon, with no added salt throughout. These squares are the real deal— save them for super special occasions, as they are super addictive.

MAKES 40 BITE-SIZED SQUARES

FOR THE COOKIE LAYER

2 cups smooth peanut butter

1½ cups superfine sugar

2 medium eggs

1 teaspoon pure vanilla extract

generous ¾ cup all-purpose flour

FOR THE BROWNIE LAYER

generous 1¾ cups all-purpose
  flour

generous ½ cup cocoa powder

⅔ cup/1¼ sticks unsalted butter

4 ounces dark chocolate (70%
  cocoa solids), chopped

generous 1 cup soft light brown
  sugar

3 large eggs, lightly beaten

4½ ounces milk chocolate chips

FOR THE MACAROON LAYER

3 large egg whites

4 cups dried unsweetened
  coconut

¼ cup superfine sugar

1 teaspoon pure vanilla extract

1 Preheat the oven to 325°F. Line the bottom and sides of a
12 x 8-inch pan with parchment paper.

2 For the cookie layer, beat the peanut butter and sugar together
until smooth. Beat the eggs in one at a time, then the vanilla. Add
the flour and beat until just incorporated. Press the dough into an
even layer in the bottom of the prepared pan. Set aside.

3 For the brownie layer, combine the flour and cocoa powder in
a medium bowl, then set aside. Melt the butter and chopped
chocolate in a saucepan over medium heat, stirring, until smooth.
Remove from the heat, let cool slightly, then stir in the sugar.
Mix in the eggs until combined. Stir in the flour mixture, then the
chocolate chips until just combined. Pour the brownie mix over
the cookie layer and spread to the edges.

4 For the macaroon layer, whisk the egg whites in a large bowl until
frothy. Toss the coconut, sugar, and vanilla together with your
hands in a separate bowl. Add the egg whites and stir until the
coconut mixture is coated. Scatter the coconut mixture in an even
layer to completely cover the brownie layer.

5 Bake for 1 hour until the top layer is golden and the pan has a
gentle wobble when shaken. (You can't use the knife insertion test
here—if a knife comes out clean the bars are overbaked.) If the
coconut is darkening too much, cover it lightly with foil.

6 Transfer the pan to a wire rack and let cool completely, preferably
overnight. Lift it out of the pan and peel away the paper. Trim the
bar with a sharp knife to make neat edges and cut into 40 very
small squares, about 1½ inch square.

Store for 7 days in an airtight container at room temperature. Not
suitable for freezing.

2

3

Carrots and pumpkin are both rich sources of beta-carotene—a protective antioxidant—and contain 0% fat. These bars provide plenty of added vitamins, minerals, and fiber. Quick and easy to make, they are great for packed lunches and picnics or to have on the go. I have swirled an optional cream cheese frosting into the bars, before baking them, for added flavor, and which means they can also be stored in the refrigerator and transported at room temperature.

Pumpkin & Carrot Bars

MAKES 16 BARS

2¼ cups all-purpose flour

2 teaspoons baking soda

2 teaspoons ground cinnamon

1 teaspoon ground ginger

1 teaspoon ground nutmeg

⅔ cup sunflower oil

3 large eggs

generous 1¼ cups soft light
   brown sugar

1 x can (14 ounce) pumpkin puree

¾ cup grated carrot

FOR THE TOPPING

½ cup cream cheese, room
   temperature

generous ¼ cup superfine sugar

2 teaspoons vanilla extract

1 Preheat the oven to 350°F. Line the bottom and sides of a 12 x 8-inch pan with parchment paper.

2 Combine the flour, baking soda, and spices together in a bowl and set aside. Combine the oil, eggs, and sugar until smooth. Stir in the flour mixture, followed by the pumpkin puree and grated carrot. Pour into the prepared pan.

3 For the cream cheese frosting, beat the ingredients together until smooth. Drop spoonfuls over the carrot and pumpkin batter and use a knife to swirl.

4 Bake for 25–30 minutes until a knife inserted comes out clean. Remove from the oven. Let cool, then cut into 16 bars.

Store for 3–5 days in an airtight container in the refrigerator. Suitable for freezing.

Moist and delicious Pumpkin and Carrot Bars.

Ginger is a flowering plant with a distinctive rhizome—and the root part has been used for culinary and ayurvedic purposes for centuries. It has a distinctive flavor, rich in B vitamins, iron, and manganese, which is essential for development, metabolism, and as part of the body's antioxidant process. Ginger is well known to combat nausea—especially morning sickness and sea sickness. It can be productive in stimulating digestion, absorption, and elimination, adding a boost to the body's natural metabolism. This shortbread includes fresh and crystallized ginger for a double hit, and is made with whole wheat flour for increased fiber. This shortbread improves with keeping, but it is essential not to overmix it—this is one where the magic really does happen in the oven. If it is overmixed, it is like a brick, and you could build houses with it!

ginger shortbread

MAKES 16 SQUARES

1¾ cups soft dark brown sugar

1½ cups/3 sticks unsalted butter, softened

1 level teaspoon baking soda

1½ inch piece of ginger, peeled and grated

1½ ounces chopped crystallized ginger

3¾ cups whole wheat flour

demerara sugar, for sprinkling

1 Preheat the oven to 325°F. Line the bottom and sides of a 12 x 8-inch pan with parchment paper.

2 Put the sugar, butter, baking soda, and both gingers in a bowl and stir with a wooden spoon until just mixed (do not beat). Add the flour and mix until it just starts to cling together.

3 Place the mixture in the prepared pan, press down firmly, and level the surface with the back of a metal spoon. Sprinkle liberally with demerara sugar and press lightly with the back of the spoon again.

4 Bake on the middle rack of the oven for about 1 hour until the shortbread is dark brown, firm in the center, and beginning to shrink away from the side of the pan.

5 Let cool in the pan for 10 minutes, then cut into 16 squares with a sharp knife. Leave for a further 15 minutes, then turn out onto a wire rack to cool completely.

Store for up to 7 days in an airtight container at room temperature. Not suitable for freezing.

2

3

Enjoy a double hit of ginger with these Ginger Shortbread Squares.

Cakes

"If I knew you were coming I'd have baked a cake!" and more often than not—I would! Baking a cake for someone—friends or family, work colleagues, or charity event—is a wonderful, pleasurable thing to do. It fills you with self-pride, a sense of achievement, and builds confidence. In this chapter I have included a selection of wonderful delicious, nutritious cakes to bake for every occasion, to have on the go, and enjoy at any time of the day. Packed full of additional nutritional ingredients to offer variety, flavor, texture, and choice, these cakes range from very simple batter or loaf cakes for the beginner to more technically challenging, roulades and layered cakes with fillings and frostings for the more adventurous baker.

Carrot Cake with Orange Cream Cheese Frosting & Walnut Praline

This is the recipe I created for the wedding of Pierce Brosnan and Keely Shaye Smith. It is wonderfully moist, with a delicious blend of carrots, fruit, and spices. Because the cake is made with sunflower oil, it is naturally dairy-free and can be served chilled. I have decorated it here with a velvet soft cream cheese frosting and caramelized walnut praline for added flavor, texture, sweetness, and crunch.

MAKES AN 8 INCH ROUND CAKE

4 large eggs

1¼ cups sunflower oil

¾ cup superfine sugar

¾ cup soft light brown sugar

2⅔ cups all-purpose flour

1 tablespoon ground cinnamon

2 teaspoons ground nutmeg

2 teaspoons baking soda

1½ ounces stem ginger in syrup, drained

grated zest of 2 oranges

grated zest of 2 lemons

scant 1 cup walnuts, chopped

generous 1 cup dried unsweetened coconut

1½ cups golden raisins, soaked in scant ¼ cup rum for 1 hour

12 ounces carrots, peeled and grated

FOR THE CREAM CHEESE FROSTING

⅓ cup/¾ stick unsalted butter, slightly softened

3¼ cups powdered sugar

¾ cup full fat cream cheese, chilled

grated zest of 1 orange

FOR THE WALNUT PRALINE

¾ cup superfine sugar

¾ cup walnuts, roughly chopped and toasted (see page 94 for how to toast nuts)

FOR THE SYRUP

¾ cup soft light brown sugar

juice of 2 lemons

juice of 2 oranges

VARIATION

Replace the orange zest with 1 tablespoon vanilla bean paste for a vanilla cream cheese frosting. Or use a dairy-free buttercream made from soy spread and powdered sugar flavored with fresh orange zest for a totally dairy-free cake.

1 Preheat the oven to 300°F. Line the bottom and sides of a deep sided 8-inch cake pan with parchment paper.

2 Blend together the eggs, oil, and sugars until well mixed. In a separate bowl, sift the flour, spices, and baking soda together and stir into the oil mixture to create a smooth batter.

3 Add the remaining ingredients until well mixed and spoon into the prepared cake pan. Bake for 2 hours until well risen, golden brown, and a knife inserted in the center comes out clean.

4 As soon as the cake is in the oven, prepare the syrup. Measure the ingredients in a bowl and stir until dissolved.

5 As soon as the cake is baked, place it on a wire rack. Pierce the cake all over with a skewer, and pour over all of the syrup. Let the cake completely cool in the pan.

6 To make the cream cheese frosting, blend the butter with the powdered sugar to resemble fine breadcrumbs. Add the chilled cream cheese and beat until smooth. Stir in the orange zest.

7 To make the praline, line a baking sheet with parchment paper. Put the sugar in a heavy-based pan over medium heat until the sugar melts and turns a warm caramel color. Add the toasted walnuts, stir until well coated, then transfer to the prepared baking sheet. Let cool, then blend in a food processor or blender, or chop with a knife, into small bite-sized pieces.

8 Turn the cooled cake out of the pan and use a palette knife to cover the top and sides of the cake with the cream cheese frosting. Use a palette knife to professionally smooth the sides of the cake. Sprinkle the top with the walnut praline and refrigerate to set.

Store for up to 7 days in an airtight container in the refrigerator. Serve at room temperature. Suitable for freezing.

CREAM CHEESE FROSTING

WALNUT PRALINE

6

7

CAKES

ASSEMBLING THE CAKE

8

Dried fruits have a high concentration of natural fruit sugar and offer nutrients, such as minerals and fiber, to cakes and other baked goods. In this chocolate cake, the prunes add texture, help keep the cake moist, and add natural sweetness, so I have reduced the sugar overall and used ground almonds, so this cake is also gluten-free.

Chocolate Cake with Prunes

MAKES AN 8-INCH ROUND CAKE

1 cup softened ready-to-eat prunes, pitted

4 tablespoons water

2 teaspoons vanilla extract

½ cup/1 stick unsalted butter, plus extra for greasing

5½ ounces dark chocolate (70% cocoa solids), broken into pieces

¾ cup superfine sugar

4 large eggs – 2 whole and 2 separated

1¼ cups ground almonds

cocoa powder, for dusting

1 Preheat the oven to 325°F. Gently stew the prunes with the water and vanilla extract over low heat until hot. Remove from the heat, cover, and allow to absorb the liquid. Blend the entire contents in a food processor or blender to make a smooth paste.

2 Grease the bottom and sides of an 8-inch springform cake pan. Line the base with parchment paper and dust the sides with cocoa powder.

3 Melt the butter and chocolate together in a heatproof bowl over a pan of simmering water. Stir in the prune paste.

4 Whisk the sugar, eggs, and egg yolks together until thick, pale, and doubled in volume. Fold the chocolate mixture into the egg mixture, then sift in the ground almonds. Fold until well combined. Whisk the remaining 2 egg whites until stiff but not dry. Gently fold into the cake batter, one-third at a time.

5 Spoon the batter into the prepared pan and bake for 20–25 minutes until the cake has crusted over. Remove from the oven and transfer to a wire rack. Let the cake completely cool in the pan—it will sink back and likely crack as it cools. Chill the cake until firm for easier handling.

6 Remove the cake from the pan, dust with additional cocoa powder, and let it come up to room temperature before serving.

Best eaten on the day it is made, although will keep for 2–3 days at room temperature, loosely covered. Not suitable for freezing.

This is the go-to favorite cake in our house. I developed this recipe with Her Majesty the Queen in mind. It combines dates with apples, fresh lemon, and ginger. The combination of brown sugars results in a rich, caramelized flavor, which balances well with the acidity of the apples and lemon. The apples provide natural sweetness and are a great source of fiber.

Queen Elizabeth Date Cake

MAKES AN 8-INCH ROUND CAKE

generous ¾ cup/1¾ sticks unsalted butter

scant ¾ cup light brown muscovado sugar

scant ¾ cup dark muscovado sugar

1½ cups Medjool dates (I use 12), each one pitted and roughly chopped into 4 pieces

¾ cup golden raisins

2 large eggs

generous 1¾ cups self-rising flour

9 ounces Granny Smith or Braeburn apples, peeled, cored, and grated (I tend to use 2 medium-large size apples. It is OK if it is just over 9 ounces, this will just make the cake more moist)

grated zest of 2 lemons

1 inch piece of ginger, peeled and grated

1 Preheat the oven to 325°F. Line the bottom and sides of an 8-inch round pan with parchment paper.

2 Put the butter and sugars in a large saucepan and heat over medium heat until melted. Stir in the chopped dates and raisins and continue to heat over low heat for about 10 minutes until the dates and raisins soften. Remove the pan from the heat and let cool.

3 Stir the eggs into the cooled mixture and mix with a wooden spoon. Stir in the flour until well mixed. Stir in the grated apple, lemon zest, and ginger until well mixed, then transfer the mixture to the prepared pan. Bake for 1 hour 15 minutes until risen and golden brown.

4 Let the cake cool in the pan for 5 minutes, then turn it out onto a wire rack to cool. This cake can be served warm with vanilla ice cream, crème fraîche, or Greek-style yogurt.

Store for up to 7 days in an airtight container at room temperature. Suitable for freezing.

VARIATION
If you want to reduce the wheat flour content, substitute ⅓ cup of the flour with coconut flour and add 1 teaspoon of baking powder.

Nutritious, delicious, with no refined sugar, and no added salt. This cake is deliciously moist, full of flavor and texture with fiber from the zucchini and pecans. It has an earthy, buttery flavor, which balances beautifully with the zesty sweetness of the optional lemon drizzle icing.

"Zucchini Pikini, into your Bikini" Cake

MAKES A 9-INCH ROUND CAKE

1⅓ cups/2¾ sticks unsalted
    butter, plus extra for greasing

2¼ cups all-purpose flour, plus
    extra for dusting

1½ cups superfine sugar

3 medium eggs

11½ ounces grated zucchini

1 teaspoon baking powder

3 teaspoons ground cinnamon

1 cup chopped pecans

1 cup golden raisins

grated zest of 2 lemons

½ cup chopped toasted pecans
    (see page 94 for how to toast
    nuts)

FOR THE LEMON DRIZZLE

scant ¾ cup powdered sugar

juice of 1 lemon

1 Preheat the oven to 350°F. Butter and flour a 9-inch ring mold.

2 Cream the butter and sugar until pale and light. Add the eggs slowly until fully mixed

3 Grate the zucchini, squeeze them gently with your hands to remove some of the moisture, then add to the creamed mixture.

4 In a separate bowl, measure and mix the flour, baking powder, and cinnamon and gently fold into the creamed batter. Stir in the pecans, raisins, and lemon zest.

5 Spoon the batter into the prepared pan and bake in the oven for 50–60 minutes until golden, firm to the touch, and a knife inserted in the center comes out clean. Transfer to a wire rack and let cool for 10 minutes in the pan before turning out to cool completely.

6 To make the drizzle, sift the powdered sugar into a bowl and add the lemon juice through a small strainer. Mix and adjust to the right consistency. Spoon into a pastry bag and snip the end. Drizzle the icing over the cake and decorate with toasted, chopped pecans.

Store for 3–5 days, covered, at room temperature or chilled. Suitable for freezing.

6

This cake is made with heavy cream rather than butter. At 46 percent fat, rather than 80 percent, the cake is low in overall fat. It is delicately flavored with vanilla and a hint of lemon. Because of the lower fat content, it is best eaten on the day it is baked, served with fresh fruit compote (see page 19).

Lemon Cream Cake

MAKES AN 8-INCH ROUND CAKE

peanut oil or butter, for greasing

1¾ cups all-purpose flour

1 lightly mounded teaspoon
    baking powder

3 large eggs, separated

scant 1½ cups powdered sugar

1 cup heavy cream

grated zest of 1 lemon

1 teaspoon vanilla powder
    (or 2 teaspoons vanilla
    bean paste)

vanilla sugar, for dusting

1 Preheat the oven to 350°F. Grease and line the bottom and sides of an 8-inch round springform cake pan.

2 Sift together the flour and baking powder. Place the egg yolks and sugar together in a bowl and whisk until thick and aerated. Beat in the cream slowly until just mixed, but do not overbeat. Fold in the flour, lemon zest, and vanilla powder.

3 Whisk the egg whites until they reach the soft peak stage and fold into the cake batter with a metal spoon. Pour the batter into the prepared pan and place in the oven. Immediately reduce the temperature to 325°F and bake for 50–60 minutes until risen, golden brown, and a skewer inserted in the center comes out clean.

4 Remove from the oven and transfer to a wire rack. Let cool for 10 minutes in the pan, then turn out and let cool completely. Dust with vanilla sugar.

Best eaten on the day it is made. Not suitable for freezing.

For those on a gluten-free diet, cornmeal is the winner. It is low in fat, less than 1g per 3½ ounces, with 0% cholesterol. It is a rich source of iron (for energy and healthy blood, hair, skin, and nails) and beta-carotene (a powerful antioxidant). This citrus and elderflower cake is served with a combination of fresh fruit and jam, for a "best of both worlds" sweetness combined with acidity.

Lemon Polenta Cake with Strawberry Compote

MAKES AN 8-INCH ROUND CAKE

generous 1 cup/2¼ sticks unsalted butter, plus extra for greasing

1¼ cups superfine sugar

3 large eggs

⅔ cup cornmeal

2½ cups ground almonds

1 teaspoon baking powder (gluten-free)

grated zest of 3 lemons

scant ¼ cup citrus juice (squeezed from the zested lemons)

scant ¼ cup elderflower cordial

FOR THE TOPPING

6 ounces strawberry jam

4 cups strawberries, hulled and quartered

grated zest and juice of 1 lime

1 Preheat the oven to 325°F. Grease and line the bottom of a non-stick 8-inch springform cake pan.

2 Cream the butter and sugar together until light and fluffy. Add the eggs slowly until fully combined.

3 In a separate bowl, combine the cornmeal, ground almonds, and baking powder. Carefully fold the dry ingredients into the cake batter until mixed. Add the zest and juice and elderflower cordial and stir until well mixed.

4 Pour the batter into the prepared pan and bake for 50 minutes or until the cake has risen and is golden on top. Remove from the oven, transfer to a wire rack, and let cool in the pan.

5 To prepare the topping, place the strawberry jam in a heavy-based saucepan and bring to a boil. Simmer the jam for 3 minutes, then add the quartered strawberries and lime zest and juice. Simmer for a further 2 minutes. Remove the strawberry compote from the heat, transfer to a clean bowl, and set aside to cool.

6 To serve, place the cake on a plate and spread the compote over the whole cake before serving.

Store for up to 3 days loosely covered with plastic wrap in the refrigerator. Not suitable for freezing.

Plum & Nectarine Upside-down Cake

Adding fresh fruit to cakes will naturally sweeten the cake, help to keep it moist, and add nutritional value. This cake is wonderful for using fruits as they come into season. Fresh pineapple, apricots, plums, nectarines, peaches, and pears can all be used. Natural sources of fiber, vitamins, minerals, and low in fat, and with more fruit and less cake, you can certainly have your cake and eat it!

(F)

MAKES A 10-INCH ROUND CAKE

¾ cup/1½ sticks softened unsalted butter

scant 1 cup superfine sugar

1½ cups self-rising flour

1½ teaspoons baking powder

3 teaspoons vanilla bean paste

3 large eggs (weighing about 4½ ounces)

¼ cup whole milk

FOR THE TOPPING

⅓ cup/¾ stick softened unsalted butter

generous ¼ cup soft light brown sugar

3 ripe nectarines, pitted – 2 quartered and 1 halved

4–6 ripe plums, pitted and quartered

1 Preheat the oven to 350°F. Line the bottom and sides of a 10-inch round cake pan with parchment paper.

2 For the topping, beat the butter and sugar together until creamy, and spread over the base and a quarter of the way up the sides of the cake pan.

3 Spread the nectarines and plums over the base.

4 For the cake, place all the ingredients in a bowl and beat for about 5 minutes until light and fluffy. Spoon the batter over the fruit and level the surface with the back of a spoon.

5 Bake for 35 minutes until golden and risen. Remove from the oven and transfer to a wire rack. Let cool in the pan for 10 minutes, then turn out onto a cake plate. Serve warm with unsweetened Greek-style yogurt, if you like.

Best eaten fresh on the day it is made. Not suitable for freezing.

VARIATION
Add chopped stem ginger in syrup or freshly grated ginger to the cake batter for added flavor.

2

3

4

CAKES

This cake is perfect when you are looking for a showstopper "naked" cake to please all palates, with added ingredients to ensure the cake is nutritious and delicious. Here I've added ground almonds to boost the nutritional content, and fresh citrus zest and coconut to add flavor.

Citrus Coconut Layered Cake

MAKES A LAYERED 8-INCH
CAKE

2½ cups/4¾ sticks unsalted
  butter, at room temperature,
  plus extra for greasing

2¾ cups superfine sugar

9 medium eggs (total weight
  about 18 ounces), beaten

4 cups ground almonds

generous 1 cup all-purpose flour

1¼ cups dried unsweetened coconut

2 teaspoons baking powder

grated zest of 2 lemons, 2 limes,
  and 2 oranges

5½ ounces Lime Curd (see page
  18), for filling

frosted rosemary and redcurrants
  (see page 184), to decorate

FOR THE SYRUP

generous ¼ cup mixed lemon,
  lime, and orange juice

scant ½ cup superfine sugar

FOR THE COCONUT
  BUTTERCREAM FROSTING

½ cup/1⅛ sticks unsalted butter,
  softened

scant 2 cups powdered sugar

2 tablespoons coconut cream

1 Preheat the oven to 325°F. Grease and line 2 x 8-inch cake pans with parchment paper. Cream together the butter and sugar until light and fluffy. Add the beaten eggs slowly, beating well after each addition.

2 In a separate bowl, mix together the almonds, flour, coconut, and baking powder. Fold into the creamed mixture until even and smooth and stir in the citrus zest. Spoon into the prepared pans, level the surface, and bake for 50 minutes until lightly golden and when pressed, spring back. Remove from the oven and transfer to a wire rack. Leave in the pan for 10 minutes, then turn the cakes out to cool completely. Chill for at least 4 hours until firm.

3 To make the syrup, blend the mixed juice with the sugar in a saucepan. Warm gently until the sugar dissolves. To make the buttercream, beat the butter and sugar together, then stir in the coconut cream.

4 To decorate, slice the 2 cakes in half horizontally, then brush each half with the syrup on the cut side. Place the first layer on a serving plate and spread with half the Lime Curd. Place a second layer on top and spread with a thin layer of coconut buttercream using a palette knife. Place the third layer on top of the second and spread it with the remaining curd.

5 Place the final fourth layer in position and spread the remaining frosting around the sides and top of the cake. Use a palette knife to scrape off any excess frosting to give the cake a rustic look. Dress the cake with frosted sprigs of rosemary and redcurrants.

Store for up to 5 days loosely covered with plastic wrap at room temperature or chilled. Not suitable for freezing.

Roulades always look impressive and are deceptively easy to make—once you know how! They contain little if any fat, making them a good choice for anyone who is looking to lower fat, cholesterol, and calories in their diet. I have chosen to fill this gluten-free roulade with a coffee cream, made with heavy or whipping cream, both of which are lower in fat than butter.

Chocolate & Coffee Roulade

SERVES 8

6 large eggs, separated

¾ cup superfine sugar, plus extra for dusting

½ cup cocoa powder, plus extra for dusting

FOR THE FILLING

1¼ cup heavy or whipping cream

½ cup powdered sugar

3 tablespoons espresso coffee, cooled

1¼ ounces chocolate-covered coffee beans, finely chopped

TO DECORATE

¼ ounce roughly chopped chocolate-covered coffee beans

1 Preheat the oven to 350°F. Line the bottom and sides of a 12 x 8-inch jelly roll pan with parchment paper.

2 Place the egg yolks and sugar in a large heatproof bowl set over a saucepan of barely simmering water and beat with a mixer at high speed until the mixture has tripled in size, is light and voluminous, and leaves a ribbon trail across the surface when lifted.

3 Sift in the cocoa and fold it through carefully with a metal spoon or balloon whisk.

4 In a separate bowl, whisk the egg whites to a soft peak. Fold the egg whites into the batter in 3 stages. It is important to fold the egg whites in gently to ensure they are evenly incorporated, but not to knock out the air, so take your time.

5 Pour the batter into the prepared pan and spread out to the corners. Bake for 15–20 minutes until risen and the surface springs back when gently pressed.

Continued overleaf...

VARIATION
To make this completely dairy-free, fill the roulade with a non-dairy cream, such as soy cream.

6 Meanwhile, soak a clean dish towel in cold water, wring it out well, and lay it on a clean counter. Cover it with a sheet of parchment paper dusted with cocoa powder and sugar.

7 As soon as the roulade is baked, remove it from the oven, invert it onto the cocoa sugar dusted paper and carefully remove the parchment by tearing it in strips. Roll the roulade up from the short end, keeping the parchment paper inside, then wrapping it inside the dish towel. The chilled, damp towel will help set the roulade in its curled position, helping to prevent cracks when it is unrolled. Set aside to cool for 1 hour.

8 To make the filling, combine the cream, powdered sugar, and espresso in a bowl. Taste and adjust the coffee or sugar as needed. Whip the cream to soft peaks. Fill a large pastry bag with an open star tip and 3 large tablespoons of the coffee cream and set aside.

9 Unroll the roulade and spread the remaining coffee cream over the surface of the roulade using a palette knife. Sprinkle with the chocolate coffee beans. Roll up tightly using the parchment paper to assist. Dust with more cocoa powder if desired. Lift onto a serving plate with the seam underneath, then remove the parchment. To decorate, hand pipe the coffee cream on top and scatter with chopped chocolate coffee beans.

Store for 2 days in the refrigerator, but it is best eaten the day it is made.

5

7

8

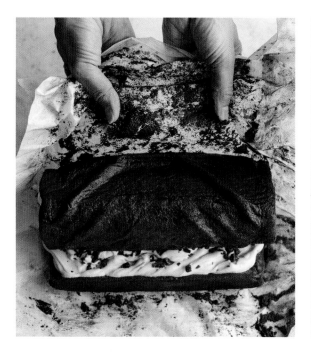

Pine nuts are rich in essential fatty acids, which are good for boosting heart health. They satisfy the appetite as well as offering texture, flavor, and taste. Combined with a lower-fat cake, this is delicious and impressive. Enjoy!

Pine Nut & Passion Fruit Roulade

SERVES 8

2 tablespoons unsalted butter

4 medium eggs

generous ½ cup superfine sugar, plus extra for dusting

2 tablespoons vanilla bean paste

grated zest of 1 lemon

scant 1 cup all-purpose flour

¾ cup pine nuts

¼ cup toasted pine nuts, to decorate

FOR THE FILLING

½ quantity of Crème Chantilly (see page 180)

½ quantity of Passion Fruit Curd (see page 18)

1 Preheat the oven to 350°F. Line a 12 x 8-inch jelly roll pan with parchment paper.

2 Melt the butter and set aside to cool. Place the eggs and sugar in a large bowl and whisk for about 5 minutes until the mixture forms a thick trail, then briefly whisk in the vanilla bean paste and lemon zest. Sift the flour into the mixture and gently fold in with a metal spoon. Drizzle in the cooled, melted butter around the edge of the bowl and gently fold in until well mixed.

3 Transfer the batter to the prepared pan, level with the back of a metal spoon, and scatter the surface with pine nuts. Bake for 10–12 minutes until risen, golden brown, and springy to the touch.

4 Soak a dish towel with cold water and place on a clean counter. Place a sheet of parchment paper on top, dusted lightly with superfine sugar. Invert the roulade onto the parchment and remove it in strips, as shown on page 156. Roll the roulade up tightly, keeping the fresh parchment inside and wrapped in the dish towel. Set aside to cool.

5 Once cooled, unravel the roulade. Use a palette knife to spread the roulade evenly with Crème Chantilly. Drizzle the Passion Fruit Curd over the surface. Carefully roll the roulade up and transfer to a serving plate. Decorate with the toasted pine nuts to serve.

Best eaten fresh on the day it is made. Not suitable for freezing.

VARIATION
Substitute the pine nuts for other nuts, such as pistachios, almonds, or chopped hazelnuts. Try other citrus curds to find your favorites.

Heavenly Vanilla Cake

This has to be the ultimate vanilla cake to include in your repertoire. It is a to-die-for-cake that never fails to impress. It is important not to rush any of the stages. This cake is made with butter and spiked with a vanilla syrup as soon as it is baked. The Swiss meringue buttercream is lower in sugar than regular buttercream. I have chosen to flavor it with freeze-dried blackcurrant powder, which adds an intensity of flavor without adding any additional sugar or artificial color. One of the secrets is the quality of the ingredients, which showcase the flavor of vanilla bean paste. The result is a nostalgic vanilla cake that quite literally nurtures the soul. Food for the Gods!

**MAKES AN 8-INCH ROUND CAKE
OR 2 X 6-INCH CAKES**

scant 3¼ cups self-rising flour

1½ cups superfine sugar

1⅓ cups/2¾ sticks unsalted
butter, softened

6 large eggs, beaten

½ cup semi-skimmed milk

3 tablespoons vanilla bean paste

FOR THE SYRUP

⅔ cup water

¾ cup superfine sugar

1 tablespoon vanilla extract

**FOR THE SWISS MERINGUE
BUTTERCREAM**

8 ounces egg whites, at room
temperature (about 6 eggs)

2 cups superfine sugar

2½ cups/4¾ sticks unsalted
butter

3 teaspoons vanilla bean paste

4–6 tablespoons freeze-dried
blackcurrant powder

1 Preheat the oven to 325°F.
Line a deep 8-inch round cake
pan or 2 x 6-inch cake pans
with parchment paper.

2 To make the syrup, put the
water, sugar, and vanilla in a
pan, heat gently until the sugar
dissolves, stirring all the time,
then remove from the heat.

3 Cream together the butter
and sugar until light and fluffy.
Add the eggs a little at a time,
beating well between each
addition. Fold the flour into the
creamed mixture. Stir in the
milk and the vanilla bean paste.

4 Spoon the batter into the
prepared pan and bake for
1½ hours (or 1 hour for the
smaller cakes) or until golden
color and a skewer inserted in
the center comes out clean.

5 Remove from the oven and
pierce the cake with a skewer
several times. Pour the syrup
over the cake. Cool, then chill
in the pan before removing.

6 To make the buttercream,
place the egg whites and
sugar in a large clean
heatproof bowl over a pan
of gently simmering water.
Beat with a balloon whisk and
monitor the temperature until
your reach 142–158°F. This will
take about 10 minutes.

7 Remove the meringue from
the heat and continue to beat
the mixture with the whisk
attachment of an electric mixer
until the meringue cools to
room temperature and has
thickened. Add the butter in

batches and beat well between
each addition. Add the vanilla
and whisk until combined.

8 Blend half the buttercream
with the blackcurrant powder.
Stir well, let stand for 1 hour,
then stir again.

9 Cut each of the cakes in half
and sandwich together with
the buttercream. Place on a
round cake board, skim coat
the cakes with blackcurrant
buttercream, and place on a
pretty cake stand.

10 Fill a large pastry bag with a
2D pastry tip and pipe a row
of buttercream roses around
the base of the cake making
sure to cover the base board
and keeping the roses even.

11 Empty the pastry bag back
into the bowl, along with
any remaining blackcurrant
buttercream and add one-
third of the remaining plain
buttercream to this. Stir to
create a paler blackcurrant
buttercream. Fill the bag with
this and pipe a second row
of roses around the middle of
the cake. Repeat this process
and pipe the top ring of roses
with a paler shade again.
Combine all the remaining
buttercream to achieve the
palest color of all, and pipe
roses on the top of the cake,
starting from the outside and
working your way inward.

Store for up to 5 days in the
refrigerator. Serve at room
temperature. Not suitable for
freezing.

LEFT Fresh blueberries are the star of this Sour Cream Vanilla and Blueberry Cake.
RIGHT Skinnylicious Vanilla Cake —FAT FREE—this vanilla cake is layered with Italian meringue and berry compote.

Sour Cream Vanilla & Blueberry Cake

Since cream has about half the fat of butter, a vanilla cake made with sour cream can be a lovely recipe to consider as a healthier option, especially if the cake is baked with fruit inside for added flavor and moistness. Here I have included sour cream and blueberries in the cake, and then topped it with a cream-based frosting and seasonal berries.

MAKES A 9-INCH ROUND CAKE

1 cup/2 sticks unsalted butter, softened, plus extra for greasing

generous 1 cup superfine sugar

4 medium eggs

1 tablespoon vanilla bean paste

generous 2 cups self-rising flour

1½ teaspoons baking powder

scant ½ cup sour cream

2 cups blueberries

FOR THE FROSTING

⅔ cup cream cheese

½ cup powdered sugar

1 teaspoon vanilla bean paste

¼ cup sour cream

1 Preheat the oven to 325°F. Grease and line the bottom and sides of a 9-inch round springform pan.

2 Cream the butter and sugar until light and fluffy, then add the beaten eggs a little at a time, beating well between each addition. Stir in the vanilla bean paste.

3 Sift the flour and baking powder together, then fold into the creamed mixture. Stir in the sour cream, then finally fold in 1 generous cup of the blueberries.

4 Spoon the batter into the prepared pan and level with the back of a spoon. Bake for 1 hour until risen, golden, and a skewer inserted into the center comes out clean.

5 Remove the cake from the oven and transfer to a wire rack. Let the cake cool in the pan for 5–10 minutes, then turn out and let cool. Chill for 2 hours, then place the cake on a cake plate.

6 To make the frosting, beat the cream cheese, powdered sugar, vanilla, and sour cream together until smooth, and spread over the surface of the chilled cake. Decorate with the remaining blueberries and chill for 2 hours to set. Let the cake come up to room temperature for 1 hour prior to serving.

Store for 2–3 days, covered, in the refrigerator. Serve at room temperature. Not suitable for freezing.

From one extreme to the other—this vanilla cake uses eggs, sugar, and flour with NO FAT AT ALL. It is wonderfully light and aerated, and is best enjoyed on the day it is made. I have layered this cake with a smooth Italian meringue and fresh berry compote. Surprisingly, it is so light you can almost feel the halo as you eat it!

MAKES AN 8-INCH ROUND CAKE

peanut oil, for greasing

6 medium eggs

scant 1 cup superfine sugar

2 teaspoons vanilla bean paste

1½ cups all-purpose flour, sifted

TO SERVE

7 ounces Fruit Compote
  (see page 19)

1 quantity of Italian Meringue
  (see page 188)

TOP TIP

To add more flavor to the cake, add the zest of 1 orange before adding the flour.

Skinnylicious Vanilla Cake

1 Preheat the oven to 325°F. Grease and line the bottom and sides of 3 x 8-inch round cake pans with parchment paper.

2 In a large bowl, whisk the eggs with the sugar and vanilla bean paste in a heatproof bowl set over a pan of barely simmering water, just until the sugar dissolves and reaches a temperature of 104–113°F—check with a thermometer or your fingers—it should feel like a hot bath.

3 Remove from the heat and transfer to an electric mixer. Continue to whisk at maximum speed for 15 minutes until the batter cools and thickens and triples in size.

4 Add the flour, 2 tablespoons at a time, and gently fold in with a metal spoon or rubber spatula until fully combined. This will help to avoid lumps without overworking the batter.

5 Transfer the batter to the prepared pans and bake for 25–30 minutes until risen, golden brown, and springs back when pressed.

6 Transfer to a wire rack. Let the cake cool for 5 minutes in the pan, then turn out and let cool completely.

7 To serve, place the base on a cake plate, and spread with half the Compote. Fill a large pastry bag with an open star tip and fill with the Italian Meringue. Hand pipe one-third of the meringue in a large circle from the center outward. Repeat with the next layer. Once the final layer is in place, finish with the Italian Meringue. Use a blowtorch to color and caramelize the meringue on the top layer.

Best eaten fresh on the day it is made. Not suitable for freezing.

This is not so much "Death by Chocolate," as it is "Died and Gone to Heaven Chocolate" cake. There is a real trend toward gluten-free baking for those with an allergy or intolerance to wheat, or who simply wish to cut down. Just because something is gluten free shouldn't make it bland and boring. This is a gluten-free version of my ultimate chocolate truffle torte. As the cake has so little flour—it can be substituted with gluten-free flour or ground almonds. The hero is the melted chocolate in the cake itself. If the cake is just baked, then chilled well, it will be stable enough to handle and decorate. Let the cake come up to room temperature to serve and you will have an indulgent cake with a fudgy center.

Ultimate Chocolate Truffle Cake (gluten-free)

MAKES A LAYERED 6-INCH ROUND CAKE

generous 1 cup/2¼ sticks
   unsalted butter, softened

1¾ cups soft light brown sugar

5 large eggs (or 6 medium eggs),
   beaten

7 ounces dark chocolate
   (70% cocoa solids), melted
   and cooled

scant 1½ cups ground almonds

grated zest of 2 oranges (optional)

1 quantity of Buttercream
   (see page 38), omitting the
   raspberry powder

seasonal fruits and/or edible
   flowers, to decorate

FOR THE CHOCOLATE GANACHE:

generous 1 cup/2¼ sticks
   unsalted butter, diced

18 ounces dark chocolate
   (70% cocoa solids), broken into
   pieces

½ cup heavy cream

TOP TIPS:
- Alternatively, bake this quantity recipe mixture in an 8-inch cake pan for 1 hour.
- Use the Chocolate Ganache to pour over cakes, blend with buttercream for cakes and cupcakes, or pipe shell and leaf decorations.
- Store the Buttercream in the refrigerator for up to 14 days, but use at room temperature. Alternatively, buttercream can be frozen for up to 3 months, then defrosted at room temperature.

1 Preheat the oven to 300°F. Line the bottom and sides of 2 x 6-inch round pans with parchment paper.

2 Cream the butter and sugar together until light and fluffy. Add the beaten eggs in a slow and steady stream. With the mixer still on medium speed, pour in the melted chocolate until fully combined. The batter should be mousse-like.

3 Fold in the ground almonds with a spatula or metal spoon until fully mixed. Spoon the batter into the prepared pans and level the surfaces. Bake for 45 minutes until risen with a crust that will wobble slightly when gently shaken. You cannot test with a knife for this cake—if it comes out clean the cake is overbaked.

4 Transfer the cake to a wire rack and cool for 15 minutes. Cover the surface with parchment paper and place in the refrigerator to chill before handling.

5 To make the ganache, put the butter and chocolate in a heatproof bowl and melt for 1–2 minutes in the microwave on high until all but melted. Bring the cream to a boil on the stovetop, then pour the cream over the butter and chocolate. Stir with a wooden spoon until fully melted and combined. Let cool slightly.

6 To make the Chocolate Buttercream, blend half the cooled Chocolate Ganache with the Buttercream— you can use more or less, depending on how chocolatey you like it.

7 Trim the top of the completely chilled cakes with a serrated knife. Use a palette knife to spread one cake generously with ganache buttercream, then invert the other on top. Fill a pastry bag with buttercream and snip ½–¾ inch from the end. Starting at the bottom, pipe the buttercream around the cake working your way upward to the top. This will

help protect the cake crumb and fill all the gaps.

8 Draw a palette knife, held perpendicular and straight, around the side of the cake, in one smooth, controlled movement. Spread the buttercream on top of the cake with the palette knife. Chill for about 30 minutes until set.

9 Fill a pastry bag with warm, chocolate ganache and snip ¼ inch from the end. Drizzle the ganache around the top edge of the cake, first to control the drips down the sides. Fill in the top of the cake with warm ganache using an angled spatula. Let set at room temperature for 30 minutes before decorating with fresh berries and edible flowers.

This cake keeps well at room temperature, uncovered, for up to 7 days. Only refrigerate if the cake is decorated with fresh fruits but serve at room temperature. Suitable for freezing.

CHOCOLATE GANACHE

CHOCOLATE BUTTERCREAM

6

ASSEMBLING THE CAKE

7

8

9

Gluten-free flour
chocolate cake

All-purpose wheat
flour chocolate cake

Trio of chocolate cakes—the chocolate cake recipe on the previous page can be made with all-purpose flour, gluten-free flour, or ground almonds. All will work well.

- The gluten-free flour will give a slightly drier cake with a more crumbly, grittier texture.
- The cake made with ground almonds will be moister, but have equally rich flavor.
- The wheat flour provides a truffle texture, less rich than the ground almonds.

Ground almond chocolate cake

This chocolate cake delivers a classic combination of chocolate and orange. Serve this showstopper for a special celebration, as it has a higher proportion of butter and sugar than some of the other recipes. By making your own soft orange curd and chocolate Swiss meringue buttercream—the filling and frosting will have less sugar than most ready-bought preserves and regular buttercream.

Layered Chocolate Orange Cake

MAKES A LAYERED 8-INCH
ROUND CAKE

1¾ cups/3½ sticks unsalted
    butter, plus extra for greasing

1 cup superfine sugar

scant 1 cup soft light brown sugar

6 large eggs (weighing about
    13 ounces)

scant 2½ cups self-rising flour

2 teaspoons baking powder

generous ½ cup cocoa powder

grated zest of 3 oranges

¼ cup whole milk

1 quantity Orange Curd (see
    page 18), for the filling

2 ounces dark chocolate
    (70% cocoa solids), for making
    decorations

6–8 cape gooseberries, to decorate

**FOR THE CHOCOLATE SWISS
    MERINGUE**

½ quantity of Swiss Meringue
    Buttercream (see page
    162), made without the
    blackcurrant powder

8 ounces melted cooled dark
    chocolate (70% cocoa solids)

1 Preheat the oven to 325°F. Grease and line the bottom and sides of 3 x 8-inch round cake pans.

2 Place the butter and sugars in a large bowl and mix until light and fluffy. Add the beaten eggs a little at a time until fully incorporated. Sift the flour, baking powder, and cocoa together and fold into the cake mixture. Stir in the orange zest and milk.

3 Divide the batter evenly between the prepared pans and level the surface with the back of a spoon. Bake for 25 minutes until the cakes are baked, beginning to come away from the side of the pan, and spring back when pressed gently.

4 Remove from the oven and transfer to a wire rack. Let the cake cool in the pan for 5 minutes before turning out to cool completely.

Continued overleaf...

CAKES

5 Make the Swiss Meringue Buttercream as instructed on page 164, then gently pour in the cooled, melted chocolate and stir until smooth. Spoon the buttercream into a pastry bag.

6 For the chocolate decorations, melt the chocolate in a bowl in the microwave and pour into a pastry bag. Snip the end and hand pipe decorations onto a chilled baking sheet lined with parchment paper. Let set.

7 Chill the cakes, then trim each one to level. Cut each cake in half with a serrated knife. Place one layer on a plate and spread with one-third of the Orange Curd.

8 Place another layer on top and spread with buttercream. Repeat until you have 6 layers with 5 layers of filling, starting and ending with a layer of Orange Curd. Lightly coat the cake with the buttercream and chill.

9 Starting at the base, pipe a vertical column of large pearls, then draw across each horizontally with a small palette knife as shown. Repeat with the next column of pearls covering the tails of the previous column. Continue all the way around the cake until it is fully decorated.

10 Peel off the set chocolate decorations from the parchment paper and position them on the top of the cake and decorate with the gooseberries.

Store for up to 3 days, uncovered, in the refrigerator. Serve at room temperature. Not suitable for freezing.

CHOCOLATE SWISS MERINGUE

5

CHOCOLATE DECORATIONS

6

DECORATING THE CAKE

9

This chocolate cake is made up of layers of chocolate genoise with very little fat. I have layered it with black cherry jam and kirsch Chantilly cream to round off the flavor. By reducing the butter, this cake has much lower fat than a regular chocolate buttercream cake. Nonetheless impressive, opt for this healthier version of a classic combination and decorate it with fresh black cherries.

Lower Fat Chocolate Cherry Cream Cake

MAKES A LAYERED 8-INCH ROUND CAKE

3 tablespoons melted butter, plus extra for greasing

6 medium eggs

scant 1 cup superfine sugar

generous 1 cup all-purpose flour

½ cup cocoa powder

18 ounces black cherry jam

2¼ cups fresh black cherries, pitted

FOR THE CRÈME CHANTILLY

1¾ cups heavy cream

generous ½ cup superfine sugar

3 tablespoons kirsch OR 1 tablespoon vanilla bean paste

1 Preheat the oven to 350°F. Grease and line the bottom and sides of 4 x 8-inch round removable bottom cake pans with parchment paper.

2 Place the eggs with the sugar in a large heatproof bowl over a pan of barely simmering water and beat with an electric hand mixer until tripled in size, pale, and leaves a ribbon trail. Remove from the heat.

3 Sift together the flour and cocoa powder into the batter and gently fold in with a metal spoon or rubber spatula until fully combined. Drizzle in the melted butter.

4 Transfer the batter to the prepared pan and bake for 12–15 minutes until the cake has risen and springs back when pressed. Do not overbake, as the cake will be dry. Transfer to a wire rack. Let the cake cool for 5 minutes, then turn out and let cool completely.

5 To make the crème Chantilly, whip the cream, sugar, and kirsch or vanilla together until voluminous and firm but still glossy. Be careful not to overwhip.

6 To serve, cut the cakes in half horizontally with a serrated knife. Place one layer on a cake plate and spread with one-third of the cherry jam, then one-third of the kirsch crème Chantilly.

7 Repeat with the other layers, jam, and cream, finishing with the final layer. Decorate with fresh black cherries.

Store for up to 3 days, uncovered, in the refrigerator. Serve at room temperature. Not suitable for freezing.

Red velvet cake gets its name from the natural, red colored anthocyanin that is released when cocoa reacts with buttermilk and vinegar. Modern cocoa processing has removed this reaction, making it necessary to add red coloring to achieve the same universally recognized color. I have chosen to add natural red beet powder to create the red hue. This cake is visually exciting, with a subtle chocolate flavor and velvety sweet cream cheese frosting. I guarantee you, the sense of achievement this cake will give you, once made, is well worth the effort. It's a super special cake to celebrate many occasions—with family, friends, and colleagues.

Natural Red Velvet Cake

MAKES A LAYERED 8-INCH ROUND CAKE

generous ¾ cup/1¾ sticks unsalted butter, at room temperature, plus extra for greasing

scant 3¼ cups all-purpose flour

¾ cup cocoa powder

1¾ ounces red beet powder

scant 2 cups superfine sugar

3 eggs, beaten

1½ teaspoons vanilla extract

1⅓ cups buttermilk

1½ teaspoons baking soda

1½ teaspoons distilled white vinegar

2 quantities of Cream Cheese Frosting (see page 134), made with vanilla extract added to taste instead of the orange zest

FOR THE SUGAR-FROSTED ROSE PETALS

a handful of red rose petals, washed and patted dry

1 egg white, lightly whisked

superfine sugar, for sprinkling

1 First, make the sugar-frosted rose petals the day before you bake your cake. Use a pastry or clean paintbrush to brush the rose petals with egg white—it is important the egg white is lightly whisked and it is only the froth that is used when frosting fruits and petals. Sprinkle with sugar, shake off the excess, and let the petals dry overnight on absorbent paper towels.

TOP TIP

You can also frost herbs and small berries (redcurrant, blueberries) in the same way.

1

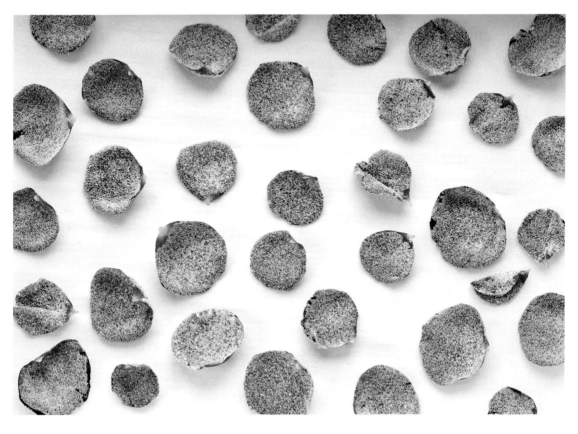

CAKES

2 When you are ready to bake, preheat the oven to 350°F. Grease 4 x 8-inch round cake pans and line with parchment paper.

3 Combine the flour, cocoa, and red beet powder in a large bowl and set aside.

4 In another large bowl, cream the butter and sugar together. Slowly whisk in the beaten eggs, then the vanilla extract.

5 Start adding the flour mixture to the butter mixture in batches, whisking well, but slowly, after each addition. The cake mixture will be thick. Add the buttermilk and stir until smooth.

6 Working quickly, combine the baking soda and vinegar in a small bowl, then fold it into the cake mixture. Once incorporated, divide the batter between the prepared cake pans.

7 Bake for 25 minutes or until a skewer inserted in the center comes out clean. Remove and cool slightly in the pan before turning out onto a wire rack to cool completely.

8 Trim the cakes so they are level. Fill a large pastry bag with a plain tip and the Cream Cheese Frosting. Place the first cake on a cake stand or plate and pipe large pearls of frosting on the top, starting at the outside and working your way inward. Top with the next layer of cake and repeat until all the layers are lined up and the top is fully decorated with frosting. Decorate with frosted rose petals.

Store for 3 days, uncovered, in the refrigerator. Not suitable for freezing.

6

Lemon Meringue Chiffon—a
real showstopper—layered with
homemade lemon curd and
decorated with Italian meringue
and fresh fruit.

Chiffon (or angel) cake is the lightest of all the sponge cakes—using the fabulous aeration properties of egg white to create a cake with volume. By nature, it has no, or very little fat, making it a good choice for those who are looking to reduce their fat intake. Don't feel too virtuous though—this cake is layered with a homemade lemon curd and smothered in Italian meringue.

Lemon Meringue Chiffon

MAKES A 10-INCH ROUND CAKE

FOR THE CHIFFON

2 cups all-purpose flour

1½ cups superfine sugar

2¼ teaspoons baking powder

½ cup sunflower oil

7 large egg yolks

¾ cup whole milk

9 large egg whites (weighing about 11 ounces)

½ teaspoon cream of tartar

2 teaspoons vanilla bean paste

grated zest of 2 lemons

1 quantity of Lemon Curd (see page 18), for the filling

fresh strawberries and raspberries and toasted chopped pistachios, to decorate

FOR THE ITALIAN MERINGUE

1½ cups superfine sugar

1 ounce light corn syrup

¼ cup water

4 medium egg whites (weighing about 5 ounces)

TO MAKE THE CHIFFON:

1 Preheat the oven to 325°F. Mix together the flour, ¾ cup of the sugar, and the baking powder. In a separate bowl, whisk together the oil, egg yolks, and milk.

2 Whisk the egg whites on high speed until frothy. Add the cream of tartar and vanilla bean paste and continue whisking to soft peak stage. Gradually add the remaining sugar, 1 teaspoon at a time, until you have a wonderfully light, aerated, velvety meringue. Add the flour mixture to the egg yolk mixture and use a balloon whisk until combined. Stir through the lemon zest.

3 Use a rubber spatula or metal spoon to fold in one-third of the meringue (foam) into the flour batter. Gently fold in the remaining foam in 2 batches using a large metal spoon. It is important that the batter and foam are evenly distributed and thoroughly mixed at this stage to ensure an even baked chiffon.

4 Pour the batter into a 10-inch tube pan which MUST NOT be lined or greased—and leave a head space of 1 inch. Bake for 50–60 minutes until risen, golden, and a knife inserted comes away clean. Remove the cake from the oven and immediately turn it upside down to cool (see Tip, page 189).

Continued overleaf...

VARIATION

Orange and Pistachio Chiffon—replace the lemon zest with orange zest and stir 1 generous cup lightly chopped toasted pistachios into the batter before baking. Cut and spread with Orange Curd (see page 18) and dress with fresh strawberries and chopped pistachios.

CAKES

TOP TIPS:

- Depending on how warm the room is, and how well the batter has aerated, you may not need to use all the cake batter. Don't be tempted to fill the pan to the top—this cake has a wonderful lift during baking, and overfilling the pan will only cause the batter to rise up and spill over in the oven.

- Do not be tempted to line or grease this pan—the secret to a great chiffon is relying on the batter being able to literally claw its way up the outside and inside walls of the pan.
- Cooling the cake in the pan upside down will ensure the cake sets in its wonderfully risen position, allowing the steam to escape and preventing a soggy chiffon. Rest assured, the cake will NOT drop out!

4

PREPARE THE ITALIAN MERINGUE:

5 Measure the sugar, corn syrup, and water into a saucepan and heat over medium-high heat, stirring gently. Place a candy thermometer in the sugar solution and stop stirring when the solution reaches 176°F. Continue heating without stirring until the temperature reaches 230°F.

6 Put the egg whites in a clean bowl and start whisking on full speed with an electric mixer. As the syrup reaches 246°F, remove the pan from the heat and, with the egg beater still on full speed, add the syrup to the egg whites in a slow, steady stream. Once all the syrup has been added, whisk until the meringue has cooled. The meringue is now ready to be used right away.

5

6

TO ASSEMBLE:

7 Run a knife around the inside of the pan to loosen the cake and carefully remove it from the pan. Trim the base and place the cake on a cake stand.

8 Slice the cake horizontally into 3 layers and spread each layer with the Lemon Curd.

9 Fill a large pastry bag with an open rosette tip (195C)

and spoon one-third of the meringue into the bag.

10 Use a palette knife to paddle the remaining meringue over the top and sides of the cake until the surface is completely coated.

11 Hand pipe shells around the base of the chiffon and rosettes on the top of the chiffon in a circular motion.

Use a blow torch to gently caramelize and color the Italian Meringue, taking care not to singe the peaks of the meringue. Decorate with the fresh fruit and toasted pistachios.

Store for up to 3 days, uncovered, in the refrigerator but serve at room temperature. Not suitable for freezing.

7

8

10

Gingerbread Cake with Cream Cheese Frosting

Gingerbread cake is a homey favorite. Melting the ingredients together makes the cake wonderfully moist and guarantees great results, time after time. Molasses has no fat and no cholesterol, and is a good source of both calcium and iron, for healthy bones, blood, and energy. The cake itself is dairy-free, and I have used a cream cheese frosting, which is naturally lower in fat than buttercream.

MAKES A 9-INCH ROUND CAKE

peanut oil, for greasing

¾ cup boiling water

½ teaspoon baking soda

5½ ounces molasses

generous ¾ cup superfine sugar

1¾ cups all-purpose flour

2 teaspoons ground ginger

1 teaspoon ground cinnamon

¼ teaspoon ground nutmeg

a pinch of ground cloves

½ teaspoon baking powder

⅓ cup sunflower oil

2 large eggs

½ quantity of Cream Cheese Frosting (see page 134)

frosted cranberries or red currants and mint leaves (see page 184), to decorate

1 Preheat the oven to 325°F. Grease and line the bottom of a 9-inch springform pan with parchment paper.

2 In a large heatproof bowl, blend the boiling water with the baking soda. Add the molasses and sugar and whisk well until the sugars dissolve. Set aside.

3 In a large mixing bowl, sift together all the remaining dry ingredients.

4 Stir the oil and eggs into the molasses mixture. Add the flour to the molasses mixture and stir with a balloon whisk until fully incorporated and smooth.

5 Pour the batter into the prepared pan and bake for 30–35 minutes, until a knife inserted in the center comes out clean.

6 Transfer the cake to a wire rack and let cool in the pan for 10 minutes. Run a knife around the pan before removing the ring, then let cake cool completely.

7 To serve, place the cake on a plate and spread the Cream Cheese Frosting over the top with a palette knife. Decorate with frosted cranberries or red currants and mint leaves.

Store for up to 3 days, uncovered, in the refrigerator but serve at room temperature. Not suitable for freezing.

LEFT This dark chocolate and
coconut cake is dairy- and oil-free.
RIGHT Dairy-free raspberry and
coconut loaf cake with a hint of lime.

Loaf cakes are quick to prepare and easy to slice. This recipe combines dark chocolate with coconut for a tasty, dairy-free, oil-free cake. Coconut milk offers a delicious, authentic taste and richness to the baked cake. The fat content of coconut milk is 20%, much lower than butter or margarine, at 80%.

Dairy-free Chocolate & Coconut Loaf

MAKES 1 LARGE LOAF CAKE

1⅔ cups full-fat coconut milk

2⅓ cups dried unsweetened coconut flakes

peanut oil, for greasing

generous 1 cup superfine sugar

2 eggs, beaten (weighing about 3½ ounces)

2 teaspoons vanilla bean paste

1¾ cups self-rising flour

2 ounces dairy-free dark chocolate (70% cocoa solids), grated (or 2 ounces cocoa nibs)

1 tablespoon toasted coconut flakes, to decorate

FOR THE DAIRY-FREE CHOCOLATE ICING

6 ounces dairy-free dark chocolate (70% cocoa solids), broken into pieces

⅓ cup water

generous 1 cup powdered sugar

1 In a mixing bowl, pour the coconut milk over the dried coconut and leave, covered, for 10 minutes to absorb the coconut milk. Preheat the oven to 325°F. Grease and line the bottom and sides of a 2-pound loaf pan with parchment paper.

2 Add the sugar, eggs, and vanilla to the soaked coconut and stir with a metal spoon. Sift in the flour and fold in the chocolate.

3 Spoon the batter into the prepared pan and bake for 1 hour and 20–30 minutes until golden brown and a knife inserted in the center comes out clean. Remove from the oven and transfer to a wire rack. Let the cake cool in the pan for 10 minutes, then carefully turn out and let cool completely.

4 To make the icing, place the chocolate and water in a small heavy-based saucepan and heat gently until melted and smooth. Remove from the heat and beat in the powdered sugar until the chocolate icing is smooth and all the lumps have gone. To decorate, re-heat the chocolate icing if needed, then brush the icing over the top of the loaf. Scatter with the coconut.

Store for up to 3 days, uncovered, in the refrigerator but serve at room temperature. Not suitable for freezing.

VARIATIONS
RASPBERRY & COCONUT—replace the chocolate with 1½ cups fresh raspberries and add the grated zest and juice of 1 lime. Top with 4 tablespoons raspberry jam and scatter with dried unsweetened coconut. Alternatively, substitute the fresh raspberries with any summer berries—choosing the smaller strawberries, or cutting larger ones into quarters. Similarly the jam can be replaced with strawberry, black currant, or apricot jam.
Lemons, limes, and oranges can all be used to complement the flavor of this cake.

4

> **TOP TIPS**
> • Coconut milk tends to
> separate, so shake well
> before opening the can, or
> decant the entire contents
> and stir thoroughly before
> measuring.
> • Chill the cake to make it
> easier to slice and serve.

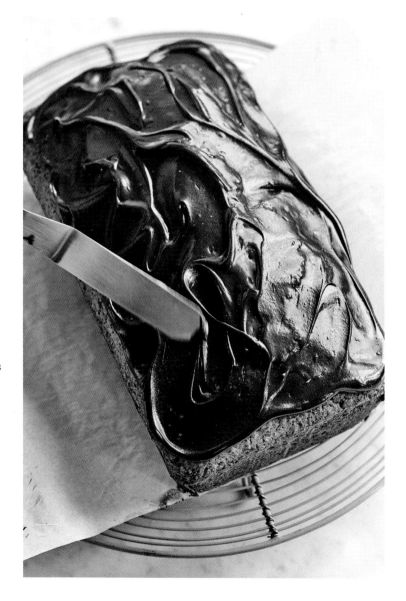

This loaf cake combines oil and Greek-style yogurt for a moist, butter-free loaf. I have added the subtle flavors of lemon, honey, and pistachio for a Mediterranean twist. Add cardamom and orange for a more pronounced flavor. Greek-style yogurt is less than 10 percent fat and is unsweetened, making this cake a healthier choice for a weekend treat. The gluten-free cornmeal adds color and texture.

Lemon, Pistachio, & Honey Loaf Cake

MAKES 1 LARGE LOAF CAKE

⅔ cup sunflower oil, plus extra for greasing

1½ cups full-fat Greek-style yogurt

3 large eggs

2 tablespoons honey (I used orange blossom or acacia)

1 teaspoon vanilla bean paste

grated zest 2 lemons

juice of 1 lemon

generous 1¾ cups self-rising flour

scant ½ cup cornmeal

1¼ cups superfine sugar

½ teaspoon baking soda

¾ cup toasted and finely chopped pistachios

FOR THE LEMON SYRUP

3 tablespoons lemon juice

generous ¼ cup superfine sugar

1 Preheat the oven to 325°F. Grease and line a 2-pound loaf pan with parchment paper.

2 Place the oil, yogurt, eggs, honey, vanilla, and lemon zest in a large mixing bowl and beat until well combined. Add the lemon juice, flour, cornmeal, sugar, baking soda and ½ cup of the pistachios and beat on a slow speed until you have a smooth, well combined batter. Pour into the prepared pan.

3 Bake for 45 minutes until risen, golden brown, and a knife inserted in the center comes out clean.

4 Remove the cake from the oven and transfer to a wire rack. Let the cake cool in the pan for 10 minutes before turning out to cool completely.

5 To make the lemon syrup, heat the lemon juice and sugar together until dissolved and reduced to a thick syrup.

6 Place the cake on a plate and drizzle with the lemon syrup. Decorate with the remaining chopped pistachios.

Store for up to 3 days, uncovered, in the refrigerator but serve at room temperature. Not suitable for freezing.

These mini loaves are deliciously nutritious—with dates, bananas, raisins, and pecans. I have used cornmeal, so the cakes are gluten-free and, with no butter or oil, the cake is dairy-free and fat-free.

Fruity Date & Tea Loaves

 GF DF F LF

MAKES 6 MINI TEA LOAVES

1½ cups Medjool dates, pitted and ready to eat

generous ¾ cup boiling water

2 ripe bananas (about 5 ounces)

¾ cup pecans, chopped

1½ cups raisins

1¼ cups dried cherries

⅔ cup fine cornmeal

2 teaspoons mixed spice

2 teaspoons baking powder (gluten-free)

¼ cup strong brewed tea

2 large egg whites (weighing about 2½ ounces)

TO DECORATE

¾ ounces pecan halves

1¾ ounces banana chips

1 Preheat the oven to 325°F. Lay 6 mini paper loaf pans on a non-stick baking sheet.

2 Put the dates in a saucepan with the boiling water and simmer until the dates have softened. Drain the liquid into a bowl and transfer the dates to a food processor or blender. Add the bananas and ½ cup of the date liquid. Blend until smooth.

3 In a separate bowl, mix together the chopped pecans, dried fruit, cornmeal, spice, and baking powder. Add the date puree and the tea and stir until combined.

4 Whisk the egg whites to soft peaks, then fold into the cake batter in 3 batches. Divide the batter between the mini loaf pans and decorate with the pecans and banana chips.

5 Bake for 25 minutes until golden, firm to the touch, and a knife inserted in the center comes out clean. Remove the cakes from the oven and transfer to a wire rack. Let the cakes cool in the paper loaf pans for 10 minutes before turning out to cool completely.

Store for up to 3 days, uncovered, in the refrigerator but serve at room temperature. Not suitable for freezing.

VARIATION
Alternatively, bake this batter in a 1-pound loaf pan for 1 hour for one larger loaf cake.

TOP TIP

Medjool dates are soft, large, sweet, moist, meaty, and firm textured. They are likely to be more expensive than most dates, but they offer a superior flavor and texture. Deglet Noor dates are more widely available and semi-dry. They have firm flesh and will need more liquid to soften them. They are generally less expensive than Medjool dates.

LEFT Quick and easy banana loaf.
RIGHT Pumpkin and poppy seed loaf
with lemon drizzle icing.

What do you do with all those bananas when they are overripe and the skin is blackened? Bake a banana loaf cake! Blackening indicates a natural ripening process, where the starch is broken down to its simple sugars—the banana softens and tastes sweeter. Do not be tempted to put bananas in the refrigerator—this will cause a "cold shock," whereby the bananas turn black, but the ripening process cannot occur. This simple loaf cake is perfect as an introduction to baking, and ideal to make with children. With added minerals and fiber, the cake is perfect for breakfast, packed lunches, and picnics.

Quick Banana Cake

MAKES 1 SMALL LOAF CAKE

½ cup/1⅛ sticks unsalted butter

¾ cup soft light brown sugar

2–3 very ripe bananas, mashed with a fork (weighing about 7 ounces)

1 teaspoon vanilla bean paste

1 large egg, beaten

1½ cups self-rising flour

¼ cup whole milk

demerara sugar, for sprinkling

1 Preheat the oven to 325°F. Line the bottom and sides of a 1-pound loaf pan with parchment paper.

2 Melt the butter and sugar together in a saucepan over medium heat. Remove from the heat, let cool for 5 minutes, then add the mashed bananas and vanilla. Add the beaten egg and stir well. Stir in the flour, followed by the milk.

3 Pour into the prepared pan, sprinkle with a tablespoon of demerara sugar, and bake for 35–40 minutes until risen, golden, and a knife inserted in the center comes out clean.

4 Transfer to a wire rack. Let cool for 10 minutes in the pan, then turn out, and let cool completely.

Store at room temperature, covered loosely with parchment paper or wax paper and foil and consume within 3 days. Not suitable for freezing.

VARIATION
Add cinnamon, a handful of raisins, or sunflower seeds to the loaf for added flavor, nutrition, and texture. Experiment to find your favorite additions.

CAKES

Around Thanksgiving, just about everything is made with pumpkin. This easy loaf cake is a great introduction to baking with pumpkin—either with a can of pumpkin puree or your own, made from scratch. This loaf is quick and easy to make, has less fat than a traditional pumpkin pie, and can be made to share with folks at the office, family, and friends to wish them all Happy Holidays. Not that we really need an excuse—this loaf is delicious and nutritious all year round! For that, I give thanks!

Pumpkin, Poppy Seed, & Lemon Loaf

MAKES 1 SMALL LOAF CAKE

¼ cup whole milk

1 large egg

1 cup canned pumpkin puree

1⅓ cups self-rising flour

½ teaspoon baking powder

¼ teaspoon baking soda

2 teaspoons ground cinnamon

1 teaspoon ground ginger

¾ cup soft light brown sugar

3½ tablespoons unsalted butter

1 tablespoon poppy seeds

grated zest 2 lemon

1 quantity of Lemon Drizzle
   (see page 142), to decorate

1 Preheat the oven to 350°F. Line the bottom and sides of a 1-pound loaf pan with parchment paper. Add the milk and egg to the pumpkin puree and stir until smooth.

2 Sift the flour, baking powder, baking soda, spices, and sugar together, then mix in the butter until it resembles fine breadcrumbs.

3 Stir the dry crumbs into the pumpkin mixture and stir until just mixed. Stir in the poppy seeds and lemon zest.

4 Spoon the batter into the prepared pan and bake for 45 minutes until risen, golden, and a knife inserted in the center comes out clean. Transfer to a wire rack. Let cool for 10 minutes in the pan, then turn out and let cool completely.

5 Pour the Lemon Drizzle over the cooled loaf to finish.

Store at room temperature, covered loosely with parchment paper or wax paper and foil and consume within 3 days. Not suitable for freezing.

Meringues

"If you are rich, you have lovely cars, and jars full of flowers, and books in rows, and a wireless, and the best sort of gramophone and meringues for supper."

WINIFRED HOLTBY, ENGLISH NOVELIST AND JOURNALIST 1898–1935

Gluten-free, fat-free, and wonderfully light and simple to make, meringues offer a delicious versatility in baking. In this chapter, I have included individual meringues that can be decorated, dressed, and deliciously devoured, as well as an impressive pavlova and layered meringue for your showstopper celebrations. Simply served with fresh fruit and lightly whipped cream, these recipes are certain to be crowd pleasers!

Meringues are by nature fat-free, dairy-free, and gluten-free—made with high protein egg whites and unrefined sugar. Adding freshly toasted nuts ramps up the flavor and provides added texture and nutrition to this cake, which I've sandwiched with fresh cream and fruits (with an optional passion fruit curd). This is an impressive cake that is actually a lot lighter than you might think, making it the perfect centerpiece for a special occasion, with fewer calories than many other cakes or desserts.

Tropical Hazelnut Meringue Cake

SERVES 8

peanut oil, for greasing

scant 1 cup hazelnuts

5 large egg whites

1¼ cups superfine sugar

½ teaspoon distilled white vinegar

1 teaspoon vanilla extract

14 ounces fresh mango

1⅔ cups heavy cream

4–6 tablespoons Passion Fruit Curd (see page 18)

grated zest and juice of 1 lemon

fresh edible flowers, to decorate

1 Preheat the oven to 325°F. Draw an 8-inch circle on 2 sheets of parchment paper, turn it upside down, and use it to line 2 greased baking sheets.

2 Place the hazelnuts on a baking sheet and toast in the oven for 10–15 minutes until golden. Remove from the oven and place on a clean dish towel. Gather the corners up and rub to remove the husks. Roughly chop in a grinder, food processor or blender, then reserve 1 tablespoon for decoration.

3 Whisk the egg whites until stiff but not dry. Add the sugar gradually. Whisk in the vinegar and vanilla, then fold in the chopped nuts. Spread the meringue into the circle on the prepared sheets. Level the surface. Bake for 30 minutes until firm to the touch. Remove from the oven and leave on the sheets to cool completely. Turn out onto a wire rack and let cool completely.

4 Blend the mango in a food processor or blender to make a puree. Whip the cream until soft and just holding its shape. Stir in 4 tablespoons mango puree.

5 Place the base meringue on a serving plate, spread with the half the mango cream. Drizzle with 2–3 tablespoons Passion Fruit Curd, then place the other meringue on top. Top with the remaining cream and curd, and dress with chopped hazelnuts and fresh edible flowers.

6 Mix the remaining mango puree with the lemon juice and zest to taste and pour into a pitcher. Chill the meringue cake and sauce in the refrigerator overnight and serve in large wedges with the sauce poured over.

Store for up to 3 days, uncovered, in the refrigerator but serve at room temperature. Not suitable for freezing.

2

3

5

Banana, Coconut & Caramel Pavlova

GF

SERVES 12

6 large egg whites at room
   temperature

scant 1½ cups superfine sugar

1 teaspoon distilled white vinegar

½ teaspoon cream of tartar

generous 1 cup dried
   unsweetened coconut

FOR THE TOPPING

1½ cups whipping cream,
   whipped

3 ripe bananas

½ quantity Salted (or unsalted)
   Caramel (see page 106)

1 ounce dried coconut flakes

" TOP TIP

To toast the coconut,
spread on a tray and bake
in the oven at 350°F for
5 minutes, then let cool.

If you are a lover of banoffee pie, but looking for a healthier option, this is the perfect dessert to consider. The gluten-free and dairy-free coconut meringue is filled with fresh cream, sliced banana, and drizzled with caramel that can also be served on the side.

1 Preheat the oven to 350°F. Draw a 10-inch circle on a sheet of parchment paper, turn it upside down, and use it to line a baking sheet.

2 Beat the egg whites into stiff peaks, but not dry, and add the sugar 1 tablespoon at a time until the whites are stiff and shiny. Add the vinegar and cream of tartar and stir in the dried coconut.

3 Spread the meringue onto the circle on the prepared sheet and make an indentation in the center with the back of a spoon.

4 Transfer the meringue to the oven, immediately reduce the temperature to 250°F, and bake for 1 hour 30 minutes. Turn off the oven, open the door slightly, and let the meringue cool completely in the oven.

5 Place the meringue on a large plate, pile it with whipped cream, and slice over the fresh, ripe bananas. Drizzle the Caramel over the top and sprinkle with toasted coconut. Serve additional Caramel on the side.

The meringue can be made up to 3 days in advance and stored in an airtight container at room temperature. Once filled, it should be consumed the same day, within 4 hours. Not suitable for freezing.

Raspberry & Rose Meringues

GF

MAKES 24 INDIVIDUAL MERINGUES

1½ cups superfine sugar

6 large egg whites, at room temperature

½ teaspoon cream of tartar

1 teaspoon distilled white vinegar

2 teaspoons rose water

4 teaspoons freeze-dried raspberry powder

FOR THE TOPPING

⅔ cup heavy cream

½ cup raspberries

1 cup fresh red currants

1 tablespoon edible dried rose petals

1 Preheat the oven to 350°F. Line a baking sheet with parchment paper. Place the sugar and egg whites in a large heatproof bowl over a pan of simmering water. Stir and heat until the temperature reaches 149°F. Remove from the heat, then whisk the meringue with the cream of tartar and vinegar until it cools and thickens. Stir in the rose water and freeze-dried raspberry powder.

2 Fill a pastry bag with a large star tip and the meringue mixture and pipe rounds onto the prepared baking sheet.

3 Transfer to the oven, immediately reduce the temperature to 250°F, and bake for 45 minutes until dried on the top. Turn off the oven, open the door slightly, and let the meringues cool completely in the oven.

4 To serve, whip the cream and fold in the raspberries. Spoon the cream onto each meringue and decorate with red currants and rose petals.

The addition of the raspberry powder makes the meringues absorb moisture and get chewy really quickly, so they are best made and eaten on the same day. Not suitable for freezing.

Raspberry and rose have a wonderful synergy, and the flavors evoke hazy summer days. These gluten-free treats feature pillowy meringues, paired with a fresh raspberry cream, and are decorated with fresh fruit.

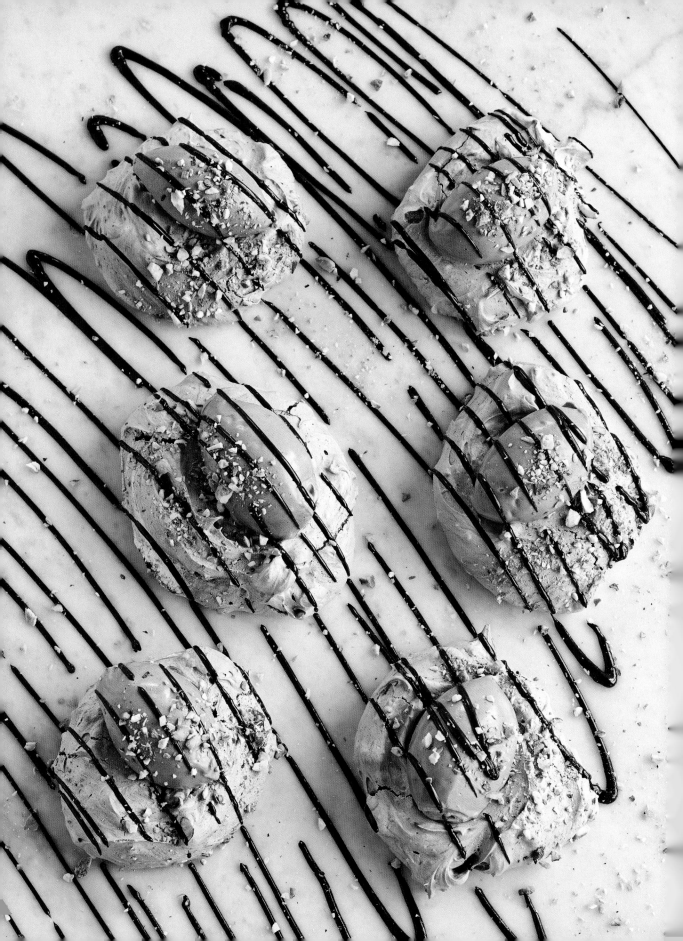

These dairy-free, gluten-free meringues are enhanced with cocoa, grated dark chocolate, and pistachios for added flavor, texture, and nutrition. I have chosen to fill these with a chocolate cream. For a completely dairy-free version, serve the meringue, fruit, and chocolate in pretty, glass bowls with a non-dairy cream.

Chocolate Pistachio Pavlova

MAKES 18 INDIVIDUAL MERINGUES

scant 1½ cups superfine sugar

6 large egg whites, at room temperature

1 teaspoon distilled white vinegar

½ teaspoon cream of tartar

2 ounces dark chocolate (70% cocoa solids), grated

½ cup cocoa powder

scant ½ cup chopped roasted pistachios

FOR THE TOPPING

5 ounces dark chocolate (70% cocoa solids), broken into pieces

¼ cup water

2⅓ cups heavy cream

generous ¼ cup superfine sugar

scant ½ cup chopped toasted pistachios, to decorate

1 Preheat the oven to 300°F. Line a baking sheet with parchment paper.

2 Place the sugar and egg whites in a large heatproof bowl over a pan of simmering water. Whisk with a hand whisk until the temperature reaches 142–158°F. Transfer to an electric mixer, add the vinegar and cream of tartar, and continue to whisk until the meringue is thick and white, and makes stiff peaks. Carefully fold in the chocolate, cocoa, and half the pistachios.

3 Drop spoonfuls of meringue onto the baking sheet, leaving room for the meringues to spread. Use the back of a spoon to make a little indentation on the top and sprinkle with the remaining pistachios.

4 Transfer to the oven, immediately reduce the temperature to 210°F, and bake for 1 hour until dried on the top. Turn off the oven, open the door slightly, and let the meringues cool completely in the oven.

5 Make the topping. Melt 4 ounces of the chocolate and the water together in a saucepan, then let cool. Start whisking the cream and sugar and as it thickens, add the melted chocolate. Continue whisking until the cream holds its shape. Fill each meringue with whipped chocolate cream.

6 Melt the remaining chocolate over a pan of simmering water or in the microwave, then place it in a pastry bag. Drizzle the meringues with the melted chocolate and top with the chopped pistachios.

The meringues can be made up to 3 days in advance and stored in an airtight container at room temperature. Once filled, they should be consumed the same day, within 4 hours. Not suitable for freezing.

This dacquoise combines thin layers of chewy almond meringue with fresh cream, apricot compote, and gloriously crunchy almond praline. As a gluten-free cake this is truly decadent, as well as visually enticing with so many textures.

Almond Dacquoise

 GF

SERVES 12–16

5 egg whites, at room temperature

½ teaspoon cream of tartar

1½ cups superfine sugar

1 cup ground almonds

1⅔ cups heavy cream

1 quantity of Praline (see page 134), made with almonds instead of walnuts, roughly chopped, to decorate

FOR THE APRICOT PUREE

8 ounces fresh apricots

superfine sugar, to taste

grated zest and juice of 1 lemon

4–6 tablespoons water

1 Preheat the oven to 275°F. Line 3 baking sheets with parchment paper, marking a 9-inch circle on each.

2 Whisk the egg whites with the cream of tartar until stiff peaks form, but not dry. Add the sugar, 1 tablespoon at a time, until stiff and shiny. Fold in the ground almonds

3 Divide the mixture between the prepared sheets. Fill a pastry bag and pipe the outline of the circle, coming into the center, as shown below.

4 Bake for 1 hour. Remove from the oven and cool slightly before removing the paper and transferring to a wire rack to cool completely.

5 To make the apricot puree, place the apricots in a saucepan with 2 tablespoons sugar, the lemon zest and juice, and the water. Simmer until the fruit has softened. Place the fruit in a food processor or blender and blend with enough liquid to make a puree. Cool and adjust the sweetness to taste.

6 Whip the cream. Layer the meringues with the cream, drizzled apricot puree, and roughly chopped praline.

The meringues can be made up to 3 days in advance and stored in an airtight container at room temperature. Once filled, they should be consumed the same day, within 4 hours. Not suitable for freezing.

Index

Resource Guide

It was key for me that this book should feature recipes made with pantry ingredients that are readily obtained from most grocery stores or online retailers—ingredients that are recognizable, offer nutritional benefit, and are there to enhance the recipe.

Amazon.com is great for more obscure items like beet powder and freeze-dried fruit powders—even canned pumpkin!

For edible flowers I can recommend Maddoxfarmorganics.co.uk

Acknowledgments

It is not surprising that to have your cake and eat it there are many people deserving of a special mention.

Firstly to my publisher—Jacqui Small. We have worked together for over 10 years now. You are unsurpassed, admired, and revered in the publishing world—for good reason. You publish books of the highest integrity, quality, and creativity. You always inspire me to give my best, to make you proud of my books, that they are worthy of being featured in your library.

Huge thanks to the extended family at Jacqui Small and Quarto—always a pleasure to work with your team—Joe, Rebecca, Farmer Jon, Emma, Simon, and Katy.

To the team at Barnes and Noble and Sterling publishing—you have given me a wonderful opportunity to publish a book with you after seeing me on stage at the Americas Cake and Sugarcraft Fair. I am a strong believer in making the most of every opportunity and maximizing these serendipitous moments. I hope this book is an enormous success for you too.

Special thanks to Ron Boire and Faith Ferguson for all their belief and support.

To all the team at Satin Ice—Kevin, Paul, Alan, and Joyce—you make life sweeter every day.

To the dream team here in the UK—Penny and Abi—I can make it and bake it, but the magic comes from the two of you to make it all look so beautiful on the page and logical to read. Penny—please stop by any time for a slice of banana cake!

Peter Cassidy—what a pleasure and privilege to work with you—"round and brown" with happy shared memories of GX and Little Venice. My best wishes to you and all the family. Thank you for bringing my bakes to life—and eating a few along the way!

Enormous thanks to David Birt and Emma Fuller—my Home Economists—your help and assistance was truly invaluable—and not just for Pop Master!

My agent—Fiona, Alison, Roz, and Maclean at Limelight Management—thank you for all your unfaltering support. Can we turn this book into a TV series please?!!

Very special thanks to the team at William Edwards—James and William—for creating such beautiful Afternoon Tea fine bone china—the Mich Turner Collection—inspired by my cake designs. I am immensely proud of the collection and hope others will enjoy cakes from **Have your cake and Eat It** served on some of our china.